# COMPANIONATE CARING:

## AN ETHICAL PHILOSOPHY OF LIFE

# COMPANIONATE CARING:
## AN ETHICAL PHILOSOPHY OF LIFE

by

SHELDON C. ACKLEY

With a foreword by
David H. Ackley

A LIVING COMPUTATION FOUNDATION BOOK
PLACITAS, NEW MEXICO

*Companionate Caring: An Ethical Philosophy of Life*





Library of Congress Control Number: 2023903424

ISBN: 978-1-958916-00-1 paperback
ISBN: 978-1-958916-01-8 pdf

# Contents

# Foreword

S HELDON CARMER ACKLEY was my father. When he died in 2008, there was discussion of making some of his writing more widely available. As the first Leader of the Ethical Humanist Society of Long Island, and later as a Senior Leader at the New York Society for Ethical Culture, Dad wrote lots of stuff, from Sunday platform talks and public essays to discussion starters and workshop frameworks for ethical leaders and members. Also, around the turn of the millenium, he wrote a virtually complete manuscript about an ethical philosophy of life, which became this book.

**Is this book for you?** Now, there are obvious red flags here: For starters, this is a philosophical book, although meant for the general interested reader. And ethics is a niche within a niche, despite Michael Schur's great achievement with the NBC sitcom *The Good Place*. Also, Dr. Sheldon C. Ackley, Ph.D., was happy to use words like "ontic" and "processual". Way to make us feel stupid, Dad. And note I'm both the publisher and a child of the author, so this book is the next-worst thing to self-published. Or maybe it's actually worse.

So this book is certainly not for everybody. But I

can say this: Throughout his life—whether as father, husband, friend, university administrator, ethical leader, or civil libertarian—Dad was an absolute ethical hardass, never cutting corners, never accepting bullshit. He was always striving not just to live an ethical life, but also to understand what that really meant, and this book is the culmination of that lifetime.

For me that way of being was just the *Ackley Way*. He got it from his dad, and I, eventually, mostly, got it from him.

In his quest to understand the ethical life, Dad had little patience for easy ministerial platitudes or hippy slogans. He wanted an actual *explanation*, and that's what he offers us here: An ethics grounded in actual physical science and the actual sweep of Western history. The story ranges from Plato and Aristotle to Newton and Adam Smith, and on down to key philosophers and scientists of the last two centuries.

Dad wouldn't say it this way, but his story has a supervillain: the idea that ethics is mostly about top-down rules imposed upon the individual to maintain social order. And it has a superhero: a plucky young view of *caring*, primarily as presented by Nel Noddings, the American feminist philosopher. And there's a cast of supporting characters ranging from concepts of networks and self-organizing systems to the philosophers William James and particularly John Dewey, who was the subject of Dad's Ph.D. dissertation (Ackley 1948).

And, spoiler alert: In the end, the ethical rebels, organized in bottom-up networks based on companionship, caring, and uniqueness, are going to reform the old top-down ethical empire based on social obligations, control, and conformity.

If that seems a happy ending, this book might be for you.

**Why is this book appearing now?** Back in 2008, I knew few of those details—to my shame today, I'd never read the manuscript. But discussions with my Dad about what we were each working on had been a signature feature of our relationship since my childhood, and we talked many times about his various reading and thinking and writing efforts that led to this book.

After Dad's apartment in midtown Manhattan was cleared out, I ended up with the contents of his computer, and I also had printouts of other materials he'd sent to my sister and me over the years. If anything was to happen with any of that, it seemed clear it would fall to me to do it. However, with my customary intense but increasingly intermittent guilt, I successfully dithered and delayed for almost 15 years.

Until now.

My training is in computer science, not philosophy. I spent a career exploring fundamental relationships between living systems and computational systems—eventually establishing the nonprofit Living Computation Foundation in 2020, to coordinate the effort after I retired from academia.

My work usually involves building *executable artifacts*—prototype machines, using custom software and more recently custom hardware too, to demonstrate novel mechanisms or display surprising behaviors. My most durable writing in English has been academic publications describing those artifacts.

I'm still building new machines, but the work is slow, and I've got a headful of ideas that I cannot honestly promise myself I'll have time to implement. More and more I'm wishing to write English without a new demo to present; to write rants or stories or jingles or whatever might *get the ideas out*, no matter who's ready to hear what I need to say.

And so, here it is: One day this past summer I thought, Hey maybe I could use Dad's old manuscript to dip my toes into the modern world of self-publishing. To learn about ISBNs and marking books returnable and all that, before I'd finished anything I could stand to ship. Make progress on a workflow while avoiding the actual work: A classic me move.

And so I rummaged through that 2008 ZIP file, and I found the manuscript for this book, and I started reading. And yeah it was philosophy but it was *good stuff*. It was clear and readable and methodical and it made a bunch of sense. And, for me, it was rich with echoes of conversations we'd had: Adaptive systems! Self-organization! Computation writ large! Core concepts of living computation, playing key roles in Dad's argument. We need to get this out there!

So here we are.

**What else should you know about this book?** Partly because of my own unconventional perspectives on life and computation, I do have some quibbles with Dad's text. I disagree, for example, with his categorical insistence, in footnote 1 on page 21, that computers are best viewed as *inherently* top-down control systems. I see a spectrum of best descriptions between bottom-up and top-down, depending on the general computer architecture at hand, as well as its specific programming and deployment.

But sometimes it's the other way round. For example, I'm uncomfortable when section 1.5 extends concepts of self-organization, and not merely dynamical systems, down to the atomic and subatomic scales—although I do see the issue raised by the Lewontin quote on page 46. The father outradicals the son on that one.

There were also a few rough spots in the "most final" manuscript version that I was able to find in Dad's files. There were a couple of nearly repeated passages, for example, which I've only lightly streamlined for this book. And its ending is abrupt: The final section is bullet points I suspect Dad hoped to enlarge upon one day. Although I'd wish for at least a victory lap there, the story must stand as it is.

Also, in this context I am eager to acknowledge the creative and editorial contributions of Richard Hartzell, who, in addition to designing the cover, also did a close proofread of the entire manuscript *and* tracked down references where Dad's citations were cryptic, errant, or missing. Dick, thanks so much! Of course any remaining errors, large or small, are wholly on me. Or, Dad.

And one last origin detail: In all the computer files I could find, Dad never actually *named* this book. So the title is on me for sure.

I think most people do care about ethics in this world, even if it often doesn't seem so. And I think some folks would really appreciate these ideas, and I hope this book finds a way to them. My goal is to help preserve it by putting it out there, a datapoint standing for its values in our evolving collective codebase. And personally, I'm just so proud of what Dad accomplished with this writing. It's pure intellectual spirits of Sheldon Ackley, distilled and blended and aged on oak.

For this book, and for the Ackley Way, and for my life:

**Dad:** Thank you. I love you. You did great.

— David H. Ackley
January, 2023
Placitas, New Mexico

# I.

# The Dynamics of Networking

## December 22, 1997

W HAT I propose to do is both ambitious and radical. It is to outline an ethics which will serve as a philosophy of life.

A philosophy of life is usually regarded as more comprehensive than an ethics, for it provides a perspective—a view of oneself, of others, and the world—which aids us in deciding what kind of person we want to be and how we can improve the quality of our life. An ethics, while also concerned with values, is looked upon rather as a constraint, valuable but irksome, which limits us as we seek our satisfactions.

My hope is to show that we do not have to choose between what we consider deeply satisfying and what we think worthwhile, between achieving a life which is fulfilling and being supportive of others as they try to do the same. I believe we all want a life which is both worthwhile and deeply satisfying in the special sense that we want our satisfactions to be worthwhile and our worthwhile activities to be satisfying. It is only if I am right in this that we can have an ethics which also serves as a philosophy of life.

The more common view is that we can gain satisfactions and we can do what is worthwhile, but the two do not overlap very much. Accordingly, we must balance the two parts of our lives, gaining as much happiness as we can without being bad and being as good as we can without becoming too unhappy. We believe this because we have an understanding of personality, personal relationships, and nature which we have inherited from ancient times. Such a comprehensive view of reality is a metaphysics, and this inherited metaphysics shapes our conception of what we can make of ourselves.

My radicalism is based in my conviction that this classical metaphysics is wrong. Our ethics, our view of nature, our theory of human nature, our conception of "the good society," all have been based in that faulty theory of reality, and they all need revision. The persistence of this traditional view of experience derives from its ability to answer questions in all these areas from the same fundamental premises. That gives this worldview an appearance of coherence, a persuasiveness which will be hard to counteract. Nevertheless, that is what I shall attempt to do. I build upon evidence accumulated by others and benefit from doubts that have long been expressed by critics of our culture. The most outspoken of these have objected to metaphysics itself, calling it nonsensical and irrelevant, but they have confused the metaphysics which has dominated western thought for at least the last three millenia with metaphysics itself. This was understandable enough, since that was the only one they had known. But we need a rounded account of experience. We need an ethics which builds upon and uses processes at work in the world. We need a view of ourselves which is realistic about the possibilities open to us because it takes into account the way natural events occur.

Therefore, we need—and I must provide if I am to succeed—a view of the way in which the world works, a metaphysics, which supersedes and replaces the metaphysics adopted in the ancient world and carried forward in our western tradition. It is only now that a philosophy of life which does this is being formulated. It rejects the mechanistic and deterministic view of nature and mankind which seemed to ignore human hopes and cast doubts upon even the possibility that we could make significant choices about our own destinies.

Because we now consider nature to comprehend all of reality, our metaphysics will be a philosophy of nature. And because science has made such tremendous advances in understanding nature, the evidence of a paradigmatic shift in scientific theory will be the most persuasive evidence of the need for an entirely new way of conceiving ourselves and the world we live in. Without scientific support, points of view that conflicted with the established worldview appeared to be romantic, sentimental, or wishful. Now that situation has changed. A new worldview is emerging, one which builds upon psychological, social, and scientific evidence and theorizing.

My daring and ambition are, then, closely related. To describe the evidence in support of my thesis that our worthwhile activities can be deeply satisfying and our deep satisfactions worthwhile, I shall, in the remainder of this chapter, give the broad outlines of the world view which is emerging from recent social and scientific theorizing. After that I shall return to the attempt to provide an account of personal and social experience which supports an ethics which is also a philosophy of life—that supports my claim that personal fulfillment and social responsibility, properly understood, support each other.

## 1.1   "The Great Transmutation"

The coming of this new worldview was a paradigmatic shift which we know as the modernizing of the western world. The modern world appeared suddenly in western civilization and had many causes. Its originators had no revolutionary intent; even as they undermined the culture into which they had been born, they thought they were improving and solidifying it. Only in retrospect can we see that its dynamic is profoundly different from that found in other civilizations—and much more powerful. That we have not understood this is one of the reasons why we have not succeeded in harnessing its energies so they serve our purposes better than they do. We have identified and used its physical energies in our technologies, but the personal and social energies it has released remain unrecognized and unrealized. This is distressing, but there is a silver lining. If we are able to identify these as-yet-unknown new forces, we should be able to turn them to good use in achieving what is most important, namely, improving the quality of our lives, relationships, and community.

That modern western society is more energetic and complex than its predecessors and neighbors, its pace more rapid, its productivity greater, and its horizons broader, is a commonplace among its observers. Among them, Marshall G. S. Hodgson had a particularly advantageous position from which to gain perspective. Hodgson was a western scholar who devoted his life to studying "Islamicate cultures." Given the perspective he gained as a member of one major civilization studying another, he saw the rise of the modern western world as having wordwide impact, in fact as one of two major turning points in world history. The first of these was the Agrarian Revolution which took place about 12,000 years ago. The shift in the means of food production that took place then, he wrote, occasioned a massive cultural shift marked by the coming of a "cited agrarianate" in which communities achieved "that combination...of urban living, literacy, and generally complex social and cultural organization, which we call 'civilization.'" Civilizations, as compared to simple agricultural groupings or food-gathering tribes, possessed "social power" of a much greater order, he argued, and this multiplied social power acted like the vortex of a whirlpool—it accelerated events, so that what had taken thousands of years now took but centuries, and it brought those who came in contact with these urbanized "civilized peoples" under their sway, both politically and culturally. The change was so remarkable that what had preceded it came to be regarded as pre-history (Hodgson [1958] 1974, 3:179).

During most of subsequent history, the known world was divided into three major civilizations displaying a "relative evenness of historical development" (3:176): the Far Eastern; one occupying the central region from the Nile to the Oxus; and the Western or European. Then, between 1600 and 1800, a change as decisive and unsettling as that which had caused the advent of civilization itself took place in western civilization (3:176-

222), destroying the rough parity among them. Hodgson called it "the great western transmutation," and it, too, created "a decisively higher level of social power." (3:177-78) Again history was accelerated, so that now what had taken centuries occurred in decades, and, more important, those who possessed the increased social power gained hegemony over all others with whom they came in contact.

The social power which was so crucial in these two decisive transformations was institutional, and it existed civilization-wide. As Hodgson described the comparative situation after the transmutation:

> Individual Europeans might still be less intelligent, less courageous, less loyal than individuals elsewhere; but when educated and organized in society, the Europeans were able to think and to act far more effectively, as members of a group, than could members of any other societies. European enterprises, such as firms or churches or, of course, governments, could muster a degree of power, intellectual, economic and social, which was of a different order from what could be mustered among even the most wealthy or vigorous peoples in the rest of the world. (3:178)

Hodgson first noticed this "transmutation" of the west because it explained cultural changes that took place in the "Islamicate cultures" at the same time. The multiplication of social power in Europe was so decisive that it affected world history: "henceforth the gap in development between one part of the world and all the rest becomes decisive, and we must understand its character in order to understand anything else." (3:176)

Our interest here lies not in these inter-civilization effects, important as they are, but in the nature of the transmutation itself. We want to find the dynamic that fueled the transmutation. In the new, modernizing communities, just as in the urban centers that appeared in the Agrarian Revolution, there were seismic social changes—a population explosion, social dislocations, and major shifts in the way in which people viewed the world and found their way in it (Childe 1936). In each case, social power accumulated in institutions of larger size and possessing greater centripetal force, the pace of change and invention quickened, and new aspirations and technologies appeared at an accelerating rate. The new institutions created "improvements in living" as ways of doing things, thinking, and organizing were altered. Because the changes were all of a piece they had an overwhelming power to transmute.

Hodgson identified three major strands in the transmutation: the economic, the intellectual, and the social. Economically, it used scientific discoveries, combined with technological applications based in them and specialized human activities taking them into account, as a base for innovative and cumulative investment—of money, labor, and materials—leading to still further investments, discoveries, and concentrations of riches and power. Intellectually, it developed an expectation of innovation that fueled extensive and specialized investigation and a general shift "from reliance on custom and continuity, to reliance on calculation and innovation." (Hodgson [1958] 1974, 3:184-185, 182) Socially, it saw production and surpluses so increased that a new middle class was created, characterized by greatly increased personal and social expectations and a "gentling of manners." (3:185, 194) Furthermore, all these changes were mutually reinforcing, and change became cumulative. The investment of time, labor, money, and inventiveness became so great that it achieved "critical mass" and could be stopped by neither internal nor external forces (3:182-184).

The changes were personal and intellectual as well as institutional. The transmutation rested in and led to a thoroughgoing revision of personal practices, values, and beliefs, as people came to view themselves differently and to describe their place in the world in ways that could not have been imagined in the Middle Ages. Thrift, industry, "regular" habits, and ambition emerged as personal virtues and "enlightened self-interest" as a social one; all of them had been either condemned or defined in an entirely different way in the medieval world. It was not that moral and intellectual conceptions were intentionally altered to be made pertinent to new ways of organizing economic, political, and social life; rather, each change produced and was reinforced by the others. Philosophical and moral viewpoints both reflected and animated social, political, and economic activities. Shifts in one area affected all others as people worked out new ways to carry on everyday activities, to perceive the world and their place in it, and to relate to others.

Our "modern western world" has its distinctive features, perspective, focus, and assessments, but the most striking feature of the culture Hodgson detected as the product of the Great Transmutation was the concomitant appearance of personal freedom and social power. Traditional theories always treat these as necessarily in conflict, and even today "communitarians" debate "liberals," the former accusing the latter of furthering personal freedom at the expense of social obligations, the latter accusing the former of supporting repressive social institutions at the expense of personal freedom and happiness. Their differences are great, but more significant is the point on which they agree—that the demands of personal freedom and social cohesiveness are, and must be, in conflict. They assert, in effect, that Hodgson could not have observed what he claimed to see. At their most moderate, both communitarians and liberals call for a balance between personal freedom and loyalty to basic common aims and values.

But Hodgson was correct in his observations, both that the modernizing world featured an increase in both personal freedom and social power and that each trend furthered the other, that is, greater social power increased the freedom of individuals and their freedom increased social power. This is not to deny that the two conflict in many ways and many settings today, but this, I shall maintain, is because we are being held back by conceptions of personality and "the good society" carried over from pre-modern days, when theorists accepted the conflict as inevitable. Neither communitarians nor liberals, holding these pre-modern views, will be able to win the debate they are carrying on. Only a view which reconciles personal and community values will prove satisfactory.

This is difficult to see even now, and it was more difficult earlier in the modernizing process. The energies being released in the modern world were different from those observable in pre-modern societies and therefore described in classical social theory. Those who tried to explain what was going on in modern Europe lacked applicable theories. What they beheld was mysterious.

## 1.2   "The Invisible Hand"

This is evident in both social and scientific theories that were developed to explain what was going on in the modernizing world. The observers were constricted in their explanations by the fact that accepted theories had always been "top down." They had always pictured some being or force which gave order to nature and guided history. The book of Genesis was one of the powerful tales illustrating this point of view. Its literal truth has been debated, but even those who dispute its details accept its theoretical structure, which pictured an all-powerful being or force bringing order into chaos. Following the same pattern, Plato, in an entirely different culture, described a Demiurge acting upon chaotic stuff to bring order into the universe. Newton accepted this tradition, by then Judæo-Christian, when he described "natural laws" which govern matter. Matter had extension but no force; force resided in the laws. Newton regarded the laws as prescriptive, but we know they are merely descriptive. All these theories postulated a source of control which brings order to otherwise chaotic natural events. They used what has been called recently the control model of nature.

The same model was used to explain social events and structures. Social organization was traditionally regarded as hierarchical. There is a ruler at the top who makes decisions; these filter to the bottom through the levels of the hierarchy, with everyone owing allegiance and obedience to those immediately above them. There were religious and secular versions: the Old Testament told of Saul being selected by Jehovah to rule absolutely over his people, and James I used this as precedent when he claimed a divine right to absolute power in seventeenth-century England. Plato justified a similar hierarchy, arguing that wise men should rule because only they could be just. Through the centuries this hierarchical structure was accepted as "natural." Conflicts—to the extent they were not simply struggles for power—were about who was best fitted to rule or who was the rightful descendant of Adam, or Allah, or someone else. The underlying assumption, that society should be organized hierarchically, was rarely questioned. Indeed, it was difficult to question it, for the theory claimed as its chief justification that it undergirded morality. To call in question the theory rather than a particular claimant to power was to question morality itself.

In modern times, however, it was authority itself which was called into question. John Locke, for example, wrote near the beginning of his *Second Treatise of Civil Government*, "The natural liberty of man is to be free from any superior power on earth.... The liberty of man in society is to be under no other legislative power but that established by consent [of the governed]...." (Locke [1690] 1960, 301) Locke was chafing under the rule of Charles II when he wrote that, but he rejected any lawmaking power that lacked the consent of those subject to it. Without intending to do so, he undercut the assumption that society is hierarchical by erasing the distinction between ruler and ruled. Locke was no revolutionary. He helped to forge the compromises of 1688 which retained the form of English society and government, but his words were inflammatory. His ideas were borrowed by those who wrote the Declaration of the Rights of Man in France and the Declaration of Independence in England's American colonies a century later, and in each case they were used to justify more radical changes. Locke was part of a transmutation he did not himself understand or fully support.

In this Locke was like the other great leaders in the west as it modernized. All of them knew what they objected to and some of them knew what they wanted, but none of them got what they sought. Luther set out to reform the papacy, Columbus to reach Cathay, Spain to increase its wealth, the English parliamentarians to restore what they took to be the "constitutional tradition" of the Anglo-Saxons, Newton to show the rationality of God, Hegel to show the rationality of history. These men made great discoveries, had momentous insights, or contributed significantly to movements which shaped history, but the most important effects of what they accomplished were what they would have considered side effects.

No one controlled the Great Transmutation, and this is the most significant fact about it. Whereas all the then existing social theories maintained that organization occurs from the top down, the Great Transmutation proceeded from the bottom up. Top-down movements are ordinarily planned; this one was unplanned. In fact, many of the previous major shifts had also been unplanned, as was, for example, the Agrarian Revolution, but theory had not noticed this fact. In planning,

1. what will constitute success is decided in advance;

2. a method to achieve success is identified and adopted in advance, though it may be subject to limited changes;

3. people and resources are organized to use the method to achieve this predefined success; and

4. outcomes and products which fail to meet the standards defining success are considered failures.

Marx's attempt to create a classless society is a notable example, and, even though he and his followers thought they were taking into account powerful historical forces, it failed. It failed at the same time an unplanned transmutation which had none of these features was overwhelming society and creating new and unstoppable forces.

It was perhaps fortunate that no one knew what was going on, for that meant no one jumped in to guide, plan, and "rationalize" the trends that were becoming so powerful. There was no movement to modernize the west. Though many people and groups furthered the new trends, they did so incidentally. They sought in one way or another to take advantage of the trends for their own benefit, thus unintentionally strengthening them. Even those who were most excited and pleased by what was going on did not know why the new society was as successful as it was. As it turned out, they were looking for the explanation in the wrong place. Accustomed to thinking of events as the products of planning, they looked for the source of the inspiration. Thinking of society, and reality, as hierarchies, they looked for who was in charge.

In *The Wealth of Nations* Adam Smith, who was one of the first to make an empirical study of what was going on in the modernizing world, illustrates the effort. He focused on how wealth was created and distributed in it, and his empirical study was exhaustive. He noted that, in spite of the fact that mercantilism was still the accepted theory of how nations become wealthy and powerful, in fact there was considerable activity going on without governmental control and it was notably successful. What astonished him was the fact that, when individuals were free to do what they thought would benefit themselves, they strengthened the community. "By pursuing his own interest... [each individual] frequently promotes that of the society more effectually than when he really intends to promote it." (Smith [1776] 1998, 292) With respect to economic affairs, Smith was claiming that the increased social power Hodgson pointed out as a characteristic of modernizing society was produced by individuals who were seeking wealth (power) for themselves but who had no interest in increasing social power. Always before, theorists had maintained that personal needs and desires had to be set aside if the common good was to be achieved, but Smith's findings contradicted this element of the common wisdom.

Smith had no explanation for his surprising results. He was himself an ethicist who had published a work in which sympathy was given the central role in sustaining social order. He might well have suppressed his economic study as being either nonsensical or immoral — he did, in fact, delay its publication for many years—but he was confident of his findings. He offered an explanation: the individual is "led by an invisible hand to promote an end which was no part of his intention." (292) The "invisible hand" explained nothing, of course, but the idea of an invisible hand was almost a necessity for one brought up to think there is always someone who ultimately is in charge. Even though he could not find a central agent in control, Smith hinted that, since the outcome was desirable, it must have been planned. The whole point, however, as we now know, was that it was unintended and unforeseen. Smith was severely criticized later for offering an explanation which was no explanation at all, but he should have been applauded for having recognized and accepted as fact a process he could not explain. We are only now coming to understand what was happening. Order, we now know, was being produced from the bottom up rather than from the top down. Smith's account of economic affairs revealed his inability to explain the facts he uncovered, but it was important nonetheless, for it suggested an entirely new way of looking at the way things work when left to themselves. It was original in suggesting that people, apparently working independently and without either agreeing upon a goal or planning to reach it, could achieve a unity which was beneficial and powerful.

This arrangement which Smith observed in society Darwin observed in nature. Darwin showed that species come and go and change while they are here. At the time none of this was thought possible. The continuing existence of unchanging species had been taken for granted for centuries; it evidenced the "order" of the biological world, and therefore its "rationality." No other arrangement was thought logically possible, for most people thought the plan was divinely instituted. Paradoxically, this worked to Darwin's benefit. Since the fixity of species was thought to be a sign of divine order, Darwin was free to consider the possibility that there was some other source of the order he found in nature. He adopted the novel idea that the energy at work was in the organisms themselves. He postulated a competition among organisms for scarce resources. Obviously, the organisms could not plan their response to this threatening situation, but Darwin described plants and animals, unable to understand the nature of the threats they faced, unable to develop plans for overcoming them, and therefore unable intentionally to modify their behavior to counter the threats, surviving (or failing to survive) in a milieu which was often unfriendly and always subject to change.

Darwin admitted that he had been profoundly influenced by the writings of Thomas Malthus, who argued that the economy Smith had pictured depended upon what was literally a struggle for survival because it led inevitably to food shortages, poverty, and death for the have-nots. It was by analogy to this dismal picture that Darwin concluded that organisms had to compete for limited resources, were capable of somehow altering their behavior to improve their chances of survival as a species, but sometimes failed and became extinct. But Darwin was no more able than Smith to explain what he saw; he simply described it. Like Smith, he recognized he should not have observed order because order is imposed; yet he did. The individual organism lived dangerously in a biological world that nonetheless evidenced a precarious stability. The mystery was profound. It was as if water had been seen running uphill.

This was unsatisfactory for mainstream scientists, because Darwin's description gave them no basis for making predictions and identified no natural laws at work. Furthermore, the argument was circular: the "theory of evolution" said that individuals varied and those best "fitted" to survive did in fact survive, but fitness was defined in terms of survival and survival in terms of fitness. One had to wait and see which organisms survived; then they could be declared retroactively to be fit. Some traditional scientists went so far as to say that Darwinism was not a scientific theory at all. What was happening? Scientists were contending that explanations had to use the control model. They failed to recognize the radical nature of Darwin's discovery. The organisms involved, maintaining themselves as viable beings, were creating an order which had its own unstable balance, the biosphere. There was no planning, no central agent or force, no purpose being carried out. Order was being introduced from the bottom up.

Not all order is introduced in this way. Both natural and artificial systems can be created and governed in a controlled way. Planned societies are well-known; the most centralized, i.e., controlled, ones have been successful as long as variables could be controlled within narrow limits, but have not proved robust enough to endure under a great variety of conditions. Plant and animal breeding has been carried on for centuries also, but it requires continued human intervention and has to respect the overall limitations of nature, as do also physical changes introduced into the environment, such as carbon dioxide emissions, the damming of rivers, etc. Control systems are those we are familiar with. We use them to exploit nature, to conduct experiments, to plan our affairs and guide public policy. But these systems Smith and Darwin studied were not control systems. The two theories, one of human economies, and the other of biological nature, both described their subject matter as a stable ferment lacking controls imposed from outside or "above." The order was being introduced from the bottom up.

We can call order introduced from the bottom up the product of dynamical systems, as opposed to control systems, because they are created by the interadjusting "bundles" of energy of which they consist, such as organisms or persons. The order dynamical systems display is self-created, self-regulating, and self-maintaining. The order never achieves perfect equilibrium, either for the total system or any of the interadjusting participants. All that can be realized is a precarious balance, a forever "almost falling," in which each participant is making its way as well as it can, given the demands upon it of the other participants. Together, they create a system of these participant systems which is also precariously balanced.

Our two examples can be described in these terms. Organisms are bundles of energy, dynamical processes participating in natural and historical processes—as functioning parts of an ecosystem, as complex beings sustaining life, and as participants in an evolutionary process. They maintain themselves, sometimes at the expense of other organisms and sometimes with their assistance and to their benefit. When one organism adjusts, it destabilizes others which have adjusted to the conditions harming the first one. What is successful today may be damaging tomorrow, and so organisms, to survive, must be able to vary their responses. Permissible variations are limited, but the limits may shift, i.e., the organisms may evolve over time. Everything about living things is temporary: even to stay abreast they must be able not only to manage in the present but to adjust to meet the demands of an ever-changing world. The only stability they can achieve is a dynamical, precarious one.

So also in society. Smith detected freely interadjusting systems, only here the systems were persons rather than (or, more precisely, as well as) biological organisms and the system they were creating by their mutual and self-maintaining interadjustments was an economy rather than an ecosystem. The same peculiar pattern was displayed. The individuals interadjusting with others as needed to maintain themselves (economically) were linking in such a way as to establish a system of such systems which was also maintaining itself. None of the adjustments anywhere in this larger system was optimal, either for an individual or for the economy, but—and this is the important lesson—the economy was "strong" in the sense that it maintained itself and created more wealth than other, planned economies because it was created by individuals operating independently rather than in a hierarchy. This is the lesson to be learned: there is no inherent conflict between personal autonomy and community strength; there are ways in which people can act so as to develop synergies between their efforts to satisfy their own concerns and their efforts to strengthen the communities to which they belong. This occurs when social controls are loosened so that individuals are freed to pursue their own concerns and to interact freely with one another as they do so. The dynamism which made this possible was of a particular sort, the kind achieved in a dynamical system.

I have referred to control systems which operate from the top down and to dynamical systems which operate from the bottom up. We need to know how each works, for the most fundamental changes being made in scientific and social theory today are those involved in shifting from viewing nature and society as the former to viewing them as the latter.

## 1.3   CONTROL SYSTEMS AND DYNAMICAL SYSTEMS

When Plato described reality as the working of the Demiurge upon the Receptacle, he set the pattern for western metaphysics and science. Since then, we have thought of both nature and the events and things that constitute it as the products of order imposed upon a state of being which lacks it, as control systems. Newton's "grand synthesis" wrote the bifurcation between passive and active, controlled and controlling, instructed and instructions, into all physical events. Reality could not be analyzed further: ontic plasticity was subject to cosmic regulation.

Plato was not generalizing from vast and varied experience accumulated in scientific research; nor did Newton have at hand information about the many types of systems found in nature. Newton's model was the solar system, the planetary motions of which are so close to equilibrium as to be atypical of the systems found in nature. Copernicus, Galileo and Newton found that extended bodies, whether located on earth or in the heavens, move according to the same principles when they are treated as geometrical points on a Euclidean space grid. (Using this finding, physicists have learned much about nature. It is captious, though true, to point out that physical events are not geometrical points and their environment is not a Euclidean, or even an Einsteinian, space grid.) They called the principles "natural laws" and thought they guided events in a rational pattern. In fact they thought this was what made their explanation understandable; all reasonable interpretations of nature would have to be of this sort. This was a control theory, a theory of nature which fit the control model. The biologist Robert Rosen has described the control model which lies at the heart of what is now called classical physics in the following terms:

Every mode of system description which we possess in physics, biology, human sciences, technology, or anywhere else, is at heart the same as the one which Newton propounded in the seventeenth century. However much these modes of system description differ technically among themselves, they all share a fundamental dualism, which can be thought of as a separation between *states* and *dynamical laws*. In some sense, the states represent what is intrinsic about a system, while the dynamical laws reflect the effects of what is outside or external. (Rosen 1987, 324)

When Plato claimed chaos is ordered by Forms and Newton that matter is governed by laws, they were using the control model to describe natural systems. The Forms and laws were controls acting upon matter from outside it. Still today, mainstream science uses the control model in devising its theories.

Control systems are most clearly exemplified by machines: materials organized so that, given necessary inputs and operated according to instructions, a desired work product results. Machines are "brittle": they can only do what they are programmed to do. This is because the instructions are preset and invariant.[1] Without their

---

[1] Recent advances have complicated machines in two respects. First, controls have been developed featuring feedback mechanisms, either negative, so that equilibrium can be restored in changed circumstances, or positive, so that results obtained can dictate changes in the controlling instructions. Second, machines have been developed which use data as their inputted materials and produce revised or reformulated data as their output. Computers are the ideal examples; they can be programmed to manage these more sophisticated operations. Neither change makes the machine any the less a control system. Even machines that are said to "learn" follow instructions that reward certain outcomes and punish others.

inputs and instructions, machines idle. With them machines operate, and their operations produce an output different from themselves. Usually the output consists of the inputted materials rearranged or modified by the inputted energy according to the instructions. When nature is regarded as a control system, it is likened to a machine. Such a view is mechanistic.

Engineering is the art of building control systems, and it has demonstrated considerable wizardry in performing its task. Engineers use the same model of reality science uses, but take over the control function Newton assigned nature's "Creator." Newtonian physics, exemplifying the Platonic metaphysics, is mechanistic: "natural laws" are instructions which "govern" matter, and nature is the output. Nature, inert matter following inexorable instructions, cannot be other than it is; it is fully determined. We have long been restive about this mechanistic view of nature, but our objections have been peripheral and unfocused until recently. We fretted about our inability to specify the forces whose effects were described but were inclined, in the face of overwhelming scientific successes, to doubt our doubts.

The essentials of the control model can be described in simple terms. The first to make the attempt systematically for a major scientific discipline was the biologist Francisco Varela (1979). I shall borrow heavily from his analysis in what follows, while modifying it at crucial points in order to make the essentials of the control model more apparent and more broadly applicable.

In this modified Varelian analysis the essentials of a mechanical system, a control system, are three:

Input — Procedure — Output

Each is clearly specified; their relationships are constant, and what happens is clearly predictable. Because a machine is brittle, it either works in its prescribed way or not at all. This places a severe limit on its inputs. The temperature may not be right, the instructions unclear, or the materials faulty. If anything goes wrong, the product is faulty or nonexistent. The mechanism that embodies the instructions is invariant, as are the instructions; it is capable only of doing what it is programmed to do. Compliance with the instructions is a procedure rather than a process, i.e., a prescribed routine rather than action which can fluctuate to deal with contingencies. One knows in advance precisely what the result will be. Machines are constructed and maintained from the outside: their energy, materials, and instructions must be supplied to them, as well as repairs when they are "out of order."

This model was used in the "Newtonian synthesis," according to which inert matter is controlled by natural laws. Extended things "acted upon" each other by the mysterious law of gravity, which was asserted to be a force, although "action at a distance" remained a mystery for Newton (Westfall 1977). Newton himself wavered between thinking he was describing and thinking he was explaining, but his synthesis was accepted eagerly by followers who accepted the control model as a necessary feature of science and Newtonian science as the only path to the truth about nature. Newton's impressive achievements fastened on science and all of us the habit of viewing nature and natural events as control systems. The "received view" of nature (Hempel 1964, 331–496), and indeed of scientific explanation (Suppe 1977), today is that events are controlled by "governing" or "covering" laws. One obvious defect of this approach is that it does not locate energy within natural events. In fact, natural laws are descriptive; they have no force.

This deficiency in classical physics was recognized a long time ago. Heinrich Hertz recognized it a century ago. In his *Principles of Mechanics* he noted that Newton had not described the force that was so clearly at work. He suggested that the unanswered question be finessed by restating Newtonian physics without using the concept of force. He admitted that, although this might increase clarity, it would not solve the problem. "When these painful contradictions are removed the painful question as to the nature of force will not have been answered; but our minds, no longer vexed, will cease to ask illegitimate questions." (Hertz 1899, 8) His suggestion was carried out by positivists; what I now propose is that we take the vexation seriously. Clearly our science will be incomplete until it can explain the dynamism in nature.

Neither natural events nor nature in its totality is a control system, nor does nature in its totality control natural events. A new model is required to make sense of a multiplicity of empirical data we have accumulated recently. Because the energy causing changes in events is contained in matter itself, I shall call the model dynamical to distinguish it from theories that find the source of energy outside the events themselves. Because energy is always systemic, I shall call the model systemic to distinguish it from those that find actions to be analyzable into simples. To describe dynamical systems is, however, to enter unfamiliar waters. The summary of the control model provided above needed little illustration, for it merely put in perspective what we learned in school. The dynamical systems model, on the other hand, has appeared only in the last fifty years, and its implications are still being worked out.

The dynamical systems model, like the control model, has three essentials:

Energy System — Process — Altered Energy System

The traditional distinction between form and function, on which the control model is based, does not hold here. The energy which constitutes the system is the process which characterizes it; the same energy transformed is the outcome; the reorganized energy created by the process is that process altered; the process effecting the change is what is reorganized. The contrast with a machine could not be greater. There is no result different from the process which appears as its product: the outcome is the process itself, now altered to maintain itself despite perturbing influences. In a control system, the central activity is a procedure, invariant and fixed; it has been set by the instructions, and it always follows the rules it has been given. In a dynamical system process is central: it is energy fluctuating to maintain itself. The specific process by which a dynamical system maintains and regulates itself is the system. Dynamical natural systems cannot be described except in process and in context.

The only stability natural systems can achieve is precarious. The course of a natural system lies within a range of possible courses of action. What course it takes reflects both its own need to maintain its coherent dynamism and its need to adjust in order to satisfy the similar needs of the systems with which it is sharing its energies. In this processual reality dynamical balance is achieved through fluctuations in a process that is operationally closed in the sense that its energies are so organized as to maintain and regulate themselves and organizationally open in the sense that it receives energies from and provides energies to other systems. The two qualities are complementary and depend upon each other. A dynamical system cannot maintain and regulate itself except by sharing energies with other systems; it cannot be influenced by and influence other systems except as it enters into and alters their energy processes and they enter into and alter its. Systemic integrity is coterminous with coadjustment and coevolution.

Energy, in all its manifestations, is systemic in the sense that it maintains and regulates itself by taking on a form that makes this possible. Energy assumes a pattern to be itself. Energy cannot act except in the specific form it takes, but the form, being essential to the process, a support for it, keeps changing as the process which creates and requires it changes. The energy process is flexible and open-ended: within limits set by the nature of its systemic integrity, it changes the way it performs its function in order to remain viable.

Thus form is not a mold into which energy fits, but a route it takes. There is no such thing as equilibrium in the traditional sense, namely, the stable state reached when something is at rest, for energy is aways in process. Flux rather than equilibrium is a system's normal state. In its never-ending fluctuations, a dynamical system retains its integrity but is never the same twice.[2]

---

[2] I have selected the phrase "dynamical system" as descriptor because it seems to me to be most appropriate. However, others, considering some of the same evidence but retaining at least some of the features of the control model, have already used it with other meanings. While they also find turbulences, discontinuities,

Natural events are dynamical systems and nature itself is a dynamical system. The evidence is perhaps most clearly evident in living things, although I shall show later that their dynamical features are to be found throughout nature.

## 1.4  ORGANISMS AS DYNAMICAL SYSTEMS

We recognize organisms as individuals (systems) struggling (dynamical) to maintain themselves (autopoietic) in nature (a system of natural systems). In their life processes, morphological development, ecological relationships, and evolution organisms are energy systems. Organisms are autopoietic (self-regulating and self-maintaining) processes. Francisco Varela and Victor Maturana originated the concept of autopoiesis in 1970. The word simply means self-maintaining, and they used the word to identify what they took to be the central and distinguishing characteristic of living things, their effort to maintain themselves as energy systems. By the end of the decade Varela had written *Principles of Biological Autonomy*, in which he presented in systematic terms and with supporting evidence the idea that everything an organism does it does to remain viable. I shall here expand upon Varela's thesis, modifying it in a number

---

nonlinearities and emergents in nature, they seek to explain them in traditional terms. Thus systems theory, chaos theory, complexity theory, and many other newly conceptualized fields of investigation propose deterministic explanations for these newly acknowledged facts. Relying, as their predecessors have, on the notion that events require "governing" or "covering" laws, they seek the rules that lead to and explain complexity. They are bound to fail finally to the extent they are bound by the control model.

of ways which I believe are required if the notion of autopoiesis is taken seriously and is applicable to all natural events.

Continued viability is the "aim" of all organismic activity and the test of its "success."[3] Specific organismic processes appear and continue simply because they are viable; they change as possible and necessary to preserve viability. The struggle is to continue as an energy system, not to preserve specific forms or functions; these must change as necessary when they become impediments to continued viability, or else the organism dies. Their self-regulating and self-maintaining processes are the central feature of all living things, the one in terms of which all other features must be understood.

Organisms are not "invented" or "created"; they organize themselves (are autocatalytic). We know only in the most general way how this happens. The first appearance of life is, at least in scientific circles, described in these terms. In a lifeless world atoms organized themselves into molecules and molecules then organized themselves into organic compounds which over time organized themselves into organisms. This is mind-boggling because we

---

[3] The language suggests intention, but here and in what follows such terms describe a "design without a designer," a purposeless process. The design language is hard to avoid because it is appropriate to a situation in which the processes are the same whether they succeed or fail and in which they sometimes fail. Continued viability is a sign of success but not evidence of purpose. Those who claim that the need to use such language is itself proof that there is a purpose dictating the course of natural events illustrate the grip of the control model. For them, events that are oriented toward results or end states cannot be other than purposive. It is, of course, the whole purpose of this exposition to show that nature is more complicated than Newtonian physics imagined—and therefore not dependent upon controls exerted from beyond them.

have been raised to explain everything by theories using the control model, but there simply is no control system which devises organisms. Their self-maintaining processes are the form their self-organizing takes. Once they have achieved their organismic form, they maintain themselves, modifying their processes, and the forms sustaining those processes, from time to time, as necessary to maintain themselves. This is the story of evolution.

To say that autopoiesis is the defining characteristic of organisms is to invert traditional acounts. It is not surprising, therefore, to find fashionable scientific accounts of organismic activity treating organisms (and their "subsystems") as mechanisms. Hochachka and Somero (1984, 15), for example, write, "Because they are the end results of cycles of mutation and selection, organisms are in a proper sense 'designed' systems, fully analogous to products of engineering design." And: "Adaptations...are analogous in process to factories or mechanical maintenance shops." (20) The analogies are inapt at the essential point: the organisms organize themselves; they are not designed. While many biologists believe organisms are not simply mechanical devices, in their own specialty they continue to look for the unvarying principles controlling operations that assemble a product; the nonmechanical elements they assume to be elsewhere. As the same biologists comment, "For understanding and prediction of assigned systems (whether designed by man or by adaptational processes) we need to know the *rules and principles of design in each case.*" (15) The explanation is always sought outside the process being described. This is the fundamental proposition Varela and others contest in claiming that all organisms are autopoietic. Organisms as autopoietic energy systems are characterized far differently. Four features are prominent: *Closure, coupling, fluctuations,* and *synergies;* here we consider each in turn.

## Closure

An organism has operational closure. It maintains and regulates itself through processes of energy transfer, conversion, maintenance, and use that are recursive, i.e., circular, spiral, loopy, helical. They feed upon themselves, expending themselves in maintaining themselves. Unlike a machine, which uses energy to produce something unlike itself, an organism acquires and uses energy to maintain itself.[4] In its recursive processes, the early steps prepare the way for later steps, which in turn prepare the way for a repeat of the earlier steps.

In metabolism, for example, chemical action takes place as a specific catalyst, or enzyme, binds with a specific substance which serves as its substrate. Each step either involves the breakdown of materials to produce energy or the synthesis of substances to produce materials necessary for continuing the process, and each step occurs in a chain that loops back upon itself. The substrate is converted to another form, and the enzyme then separates from it. The enzyme can be used again, either in the same way or in a different chemical combination, while the substrate in its converted form becomes the substrate for other enzymes. The catalyst is not used up in

---

[4]We could say the energy is used solely for self-maintenance, except that sometimes earlier adjustments have been embodied in structures that remain but are no longer pertinent to self-maintenance. These vermiform structures may limit current energy transfers and conversions, thus introducing "inefficiency" into the organism.

catalysis, and the products of each step are the materials necessary for later ones. Each step in the loop excites and/or inhibits specific actions, which constitute internal adjustments of the energies contained in the loop. Each action converts energy in such a way as to set the stage for the next step or steps in a progressive sequence. At every stage the process adjusts its details as the needs and contributions of related processes and its own needs change. It speeds up or slows down, produces different materials or energies, and eliminates or postpones certain processes and then reactivates them.

The same is true of the sensori-motor system. It is usually described as a sequence of stimuli and their responses, the assumption being that the system is at equilibrium, then disturbed by some action or condition that arouses it, and then adjusts to restore equilibrium. Varela (1991, 89), correcting this view, noted that the "activity of sensors is brought about most typically by the organism's motions." These motions are necessary to self-maintenance. Far from being at equilibrium, the nervous system is so far from equilibrium that the slightest triggering impulse originating in the motor system sets off profound fluctuations system-wide. The incessant movements of the organism impact upon its surroundings, and sensory "soundings" are fed back to it; the organism adjusts its motor-sensory loopings to make best use of its couplings with related processes, thus correcting, guiding, and regulating its activity. The motor activity is continuous and necessary to maintain viability; the sensory and nervous activities support it in that effort.

Still a third example is that of the immune system. The traditional account ascribed to the immune system the ability to locate elements that are "natural enemies" and identify them as "foreign." (See, e.g., Burnet 1959 and Edelman 1992.) That approach in effect postulated the existence of a massive data bank of natural enemies either existing prior to infections or assembled through incidents of infection; the organism presumably had a response tailored to the threat posed by each natural enemy. The theory was shattered when it was discovered that immunity acts against artificial antigens. Gradually the immune system has come to be viewed as a recursive process maintaining and regulating itself.

> All immune events are directed inward, not outward, and the organism perceives the penetration of foreign materials not by recognizing them as foreign but rather because the foreign elements interfere with ongoing reactions that exist as links in a complex network of interactions.... [The] permissible interactions are those, and only those, that the components of the system specify, and that are compatible with the maintenance of closure, .... self-organization, and recursive history. (Varela 1979, 231-2, 237)

The immune system does not have to have a rolodex file of antigens, artificial as well as natural; it is a recursive, self-maintaining system. It counteracts antigens because they interfere with the processes by which it maintains itself.

In each of these systems closure is achieved by processes that feed forward. In a machine, feedback is often important; its function is to maintain equilibrium by returning the system to "normal." In a control system containing feedback mechanisms, feed forward is a source of instability not acceptable to the proper operation of the system; it is illustrated by the screech in a PA system. Where it is used, as in starting an atomic pile, it must be carefully controlled at a different level. If incorporated in the mechanism—as in an atomic pile—it must be regulated by negative feedback. In an organism, on the other hand, the looping energies feed forward as well as back. Organic functions of activation, inhibition, induced fit, repression, and induction maintain the energy flow of the organism by altering the conversion processes themselves, as well as their rates (Reiner 1968, 115-17, 126-33). The process maintains life processes rather than equilibrium. Both the metabolic system and the organism attain closure through this interplay of metabolic processes. None of the systems "dictate" to the others; each is sensitive to and responsive to the others as it and they enter into each other's processes. The net result is that each maintains itself and participates in the self-maintaining activities of the organism.

Every bodily function, cell, molecule, and the organism itself is its recursive processes and the varying forms they assume to sustain themselves. Recursive loops are the self-sustaining form energy takes. The processes "that endow natural systems with autonomy... have to do with pervasive circularities to be found in nature. We are led to consider in all seriousness the traditional image of the snake eating its own tail as the guiding image for autonomy as self-law and self-regulation."[5] (Varela

---

[5] Because the word "law" has so generally been used, à la Newton, to refer to a formal force or cause, reference here to "self-law" is both unnecessary and misleading. It is the energies of organisms, and autonomous natural systems generally, that are regulative and directive, not laws describing or controlling them.

1979, xii)

## Coupling

The recursive loops by which organisms maintain themselves cannot be separated, or even clearly distinguished, from their surroundings as the parts of a machine can. Energy flows overlap and transfer from one system to another. The overlaps and transfers occur when two or more systems couple, that is to say, when their recursive, energy-sustaining sequences are joined so that the energy, whatever its form, is transferred from one system to the other or serves as a common step in both. The sensory and motor systems of an organism are coupled, as are all its other subsystems. The organism is coupled with each and all of them. It is a complex of coupled systems, each, like it, autopoietic.

Organisms cannot exist without coupling. While organisms as energy systems are operationally closed, they are organizationally open. They cannot maintain themselves without entering into other energy systems. An organism, not having someone to supply it with fuel and remove its wastes, must obtain its own energy and expel its own waste. This is so important that Ilya Prigogine (Nicolis and Prigogine 1977) uses the term "dissipative" rather than "autopoietic" to characterize such systems. In being open and dissipative, living things reach into their surroundings in a very selective way to perform their functions. Because standard accounts of individuality and relationships are so static, it is both difficult and important to make clear how an organism that is autopoietic can at the same time in order to maintain itself enter into other systems which are also autopoietic.

An organism, or any organic process, must couple with other energy systems in order to maintain its operational closure. Looping and coupling are complementary processes, each necessary to the other. Autopoiesis requires both. Because the processes by which organisms link themselves to the world about them are their recursive processes themselves, they do not become less themselves or less autopoietic in their interdependence; rather they maintain themselves in this way. This has been called the "autopoietic paradox": "the greater an organisms' autonomy, the more feedback loops [positive and negative] required both within the system and in its relationship to the environment." (Briggs and Peat 1989, 165) The paradoxical nature of coupling is everywhere. In some cases—as when one organism infects another with a deadly disease—the coupling is fatal to one system. More commonly, however, the common step is essential to or compatible with the continued viability of both systems. Where this is not or appears not to be true, as in predator-prey relationships, the system being studied is coupled with other systems, such as, in this case, the ecosystem, a system to which biological decay makes a contribution. What is "beneficial" depends upon one's point of view. The couplings are, in every case, essential aspects of the autopoietic processes of the systems that are coupling.

Because coupling is the only way systems can maintain themselves and connect with their surroundings and because every natural system couples with so many others and in so many ways, we can think of relatedness as networking. A network is a complex of couplings, and, since the only things that can couple are recursive energy processes (loops), a network is a complex of looping couplings or coupling loopings. Every organism participates in a network of systems and is constituted of a network. Organisms depend for their continued existence upon processes which, in order to maintain themselves, must incorporate or enter "into" processes that are "outside" them in the sense that they are essential processes of other autopoietic systems. We saw earlier that autopoiesis could occur in one organism only through energy transfers or conversions in a recursive process; where systems are coupled, these processes are intersystemic but still of the same nature.

Because loopings require couplings and couplings require loopings, relationships are constitutive. Networking is the process by which energies utilize other energies to maintain their systemic integrity. In coupling, the recursive energy flows that are transferred from one system to another or that serve as a common element in each are modified. Each of the systems, whether cells, organisms, subsystems of organisms, or something else, adjusts to accommodate or modify the energy flow of the other. Coupling is interadjustive, and every other natural system (event) coupling with an organic event affects what that event is. Each coupling system has its own systemic requirements, which it imposes upon the systems with which it is coupling. They have their systemic requirements, too, and they are just as insistent upon imposing them upon the first system; thus every system in a network is adjusting to and being adjusted to by all the others in the network. All change and all constancy, all relationship and all integrity, is interadjustive.

An organism is a complex of systems coupling and looping with it and with each other. The circulatory system of an animal depends upon oxygen, and oxygen cannot get "into" the blood stream except as the respiratory loop of energy conversions and transfers couples with the circulatory loop of energy conversions and transfers. The circulatory system also needs chemicals it can only get by coupling with the digestive system, and both the respiratory and digestive system are coupled with the circulatory system. An organism is a network of interpenetrating and interadjusting systems, each maintaining itself through its couplings with the others. In each coupling each of the interadjusting systems is both "inside" and "outside" each of the others. Each consists of its own recursive processes and so is autonomous, but each is also participating in the others in a specific and limited way and so is networking. The autonomy and networking of organisms are not contraries, but correlates. The organism hunts and gathers, using muscles that know nothing of hunting and gathering to satisfy hunger that the nervous system does not feel and restore tissues in these and other systems that recognize no loss. Each of the subsystems is maintaining its own recursive processes by coupling with the recursive, self-maintaining processes of the organism, which can be carried out only through its coupling with its own subsystems.

But this is only part of the story. An organism is also maintaining itself by networking with both physical and living systems in its ecosystem. The coupling here is of exactly the same nature and just as essential to its self-regulation and maintenance. "The system and the environment... have an interlocked history of structural [and functional]⁶ transformations, selecting each other's

---

⁶ The addition contained in the inserted brackets point to an important difference between Varela's position and mine (or else to his too ready acceptance of the preference for structure over

trajectories." (Varela 1979, 33) There is no organism which is not participating in an "environment" of inter-adjusting coupled systems. To express the relationship nontechnically, dynamical systems need each other in order to be themselves. The coupling is just as essential to autopoiesis as the looping. In fact, it is just as accurate to say that organisms and other dynamical systems set up and maintain their recursive processes in order to establish and continue their relationships with their sur-roundings as to say they establish relationships in order to maintain themselves.

## Fluctuations

Autopoietic systems maintain their processual integrity by fluctuating. A fluctuation is any modification of the loopings and couplings of a natural event. A fluctuation adjusts the energy loopings of the system in which it occurs so it can maintain its dynamical balance, just as a tightrope walker moves constantly to succeed in her high wire act. It also adjusts the energy couplings of the system and so is interadjustive. And, since the loopings and couplings are interdependent, every adjustment is an interadjustment. In a network this is a highly com-plex process. To use an example from mammalian life, membrane fluidity is adjusted with temperature to pre-serve membrane-based enzyme, hormone, and transport functions; solute levels are adjusted to conserve enzyme

---

function in the ontology he is criticizing and attempting to replace). Self-maintenance is a process, a function; form, structure must be and is sacrificed when necessary to continue the function. The identity being preserved is that of an energy system navigating among other energy systems which are both inside and outside it.

structure, function, and regulation; blood pH is adjusted as temperature changes in order to preserve protein functions (Hochachka and Somero, 5-6). The changes within the mammal reflect and cause complementary changes in its environment. The fluctuations are necessary to maintain the precarious balance characteristic of dynamical systems, but not all are adjustive. A heart fibrillation may respond to other needs of the organism but cause the heart to stop beating, for example.

Unlike the sequences of events in linear causation, fluctuations, occurring in networks, are at one and the same time causes and effects. No fluctuation or system can be "singled out" as either cause or effect of the others; each is a part of the systems it is perturbing. Interadjustment is much more than interaction. When systems are coupled, "their respective paths of autopoiesis constitute reciprocal sources of compensable perturbation." (Varela 1979, 50) None of the systems in a network maintains equilibrium; each is off balance because its loopings are being used by the other systems in the network to improve their own balance. Since each system is off balance, it fluctuates, thus disturbing the balance of all the systems with which it is networking, for, since its looping is dependent upon its coupling, the forces of the systems coupled with it are part of its own looping.

These interadjustive changes are sometimes called perturbations, but I have called them fluctuations for a reason. Traditional accounts viewed all causes as external, but this is not true in networks. Each participating system in a network both acts to meet its own autopoi etic needs and responds to the autopoietic needs of the other networking systems. The latter may be considered perturbation-compensating fluctuations, but the former cannot. Some fluctuations simply respond to the need of their own system to maintain its precarious balance. The eye, for example, is constantly fluctuating, even when closed; if it did not, it could not see. The heart beat is, of necessity, irregular. If it were perfectly regular, the organism would die. A fluctuation is an essential of autopoietic action. It is a shift that an off-balance system makes to remain viable. It would be a mistake, therefore, to think of all fluctuations as perturbations. It would suggest what is not true, that all action is a response to external forces. This was the classical view, which assumed that organisms are separate and maintain equilibrium. However, since there is no such thing as a system at equilibrium, each system adjusts by seeking a new balance in its looping-coupling with other systems with which it is networking. The result is a new dynamical balance in which no participating system is the same as it was before. Rather than being variations from a norm, fluctuations map out a domain of variations, and the integrity of a system is defined, not by its inflexibility, but by its flexibility in its domain of variations. Whatever balance is achieved in a network depends upon the imbalances within and among its participating systems. Organic processes all fluctuate as possible and necessary to maximize organismic balance, just as a bicycle rider alters the action of his muscles, lungs, heart, senses, etc., in order to keep his balance and reach his destination. He cannot come to rest; there is no perfect equilibrium for the cyclist. In the same way an organism's fluctuations are not actions taken by a being which could be at equilibrium and dispense with them. Rather, the fluctuations are a necessary feature of the energy system.

Fluctuations respond to the need of the system in

which they occur, but they do this only temporarily and imperfectly because they also respond to the autopoietic needs of the systems with which this system is coupled. But the autopoietic needs of these other systems are never entirely harmonized with those of its own. Hence, every fluctuation is perturbing as well as adjustive. Fluctuations anywhere reverberate throughout the network, upsetting the poised instability that exists elsewhere in the system and causing perturbation-compensating fluctuations in all the networking systems. Each system in the network must accommodate as well as it can to such perturbations to maintain the integrity of its own recursive and coupled loops. A change anywhere in either its own processes or those with which it is coupled requires adjustments elsewhere, and perhaps everywhere else, in the network.

These adjustments and their reverberations take time. The adjustments pulse, and the compensating adjustments are reflexive over a period of time, that is, cyclic. A perturbs B, and a ripple effect pervades the network. A pulse later the perturbed and changed B perturbs A and C, both of which in turn.... The participation in networking reality is pulsed, with the duration of each pulse varying from one type of organism to another. Neural nets are well known to operate in this near instantaneous but discernibly temporal fashion; in human beings, neural responses typically require 200-500 msec. The experience of "nowness" can be no narrower than this.

Thus every fluctuation, anywhere in a network, not only reconstitutes each participating system but also triggers a cascade of interadjustments, no one of which can be traced to any single fluctuation or any isolatable combination of fluctuations. Causation in a network of dynamical systems is circular. (To call the causation circular is not quite precise since each system is reconstituted, i.e., becomes at least slightly different in its processes, at every moment, so that the A that perturbed B is not the one B perturbs by its compensating fluctuation.) Causes reverberate temporally and multidirectionally. They circle back upon themselves, but altered by the adjustive responses of the system they perturb. The whole network is altered at each instant.

The reverberation is a spiraling effect in a network, a cascade of systemic refittings which both maintain the participant systems and lead to a novel resolution of forces.

## Synergies

The looping-coupling of autopoietic systems, with their networking fluctuations, is synergistic. Systems autocatalyze and become autopoietic when systems at a particular energy level are subjected to forces so great they are destabilized and re-form (ordinarily with other energies) in a system balancing centripetal and centrifugal forces greater than those found in the original, and now defunct, system.

The standard account, in part speculative to date, given for the formation of life itself illustrates what happens: a burst of energy, whether lightning, cosmic rays, or some conflagration of energies existing in the primordial soup, forced the reorganization of existing forms into a simple organism. The soup, disordered by the burst of energy—that is to say, forced out of its previous autopoietic processes—responded to catalyze a new, living system. Catalysis caused by such a burst of excessive energy involves the formation of new recursive processes maintaining themselves at a higher energy level which requires more complex organization. The recent accounts of "chaos" and "complexity" explain the autocatalysis as what occurs at a "bifurcation point." Such bifurcation points appear when energy beyond that which can be used by the precedent systems force them into turbulence that is unstable. The new system appears amid the turbulence. A bifurcation occurs when "a slight fluctuation... is swelled by iteration to a size so great that a fork is created and the system takes off in a new direction, [stabilizing in] a new behavior through a series of feedback [and feed forward] loops that couple the new change to the environment." (Briggs and Peat 1989, 143)

The new system generates energy at a faster rate, and its processes are recursive precisely because recursive processes feed upon themselves and so are best suited to accommodate energy at the higher levels. An eddy forming in a river, a soliton in a metal rod struck on one end, a sound wave created by a cannon shot, all illustrate a nonlinear organization of energies, a synergy. Organisms are synergistic. Their recursive processes lock in energy flows at rates far higher than are ordinarily found in their environments. They derive their energy, directly or indirectly, from the sun, but one gram of human body weight releases 10,000 times more heat than one gram of the sun. Using basal metabolism as an energy measure, investigators have found that a running man releases the same relative amount of heat as an ocean liner; a fruit fly, while flying, the same relative amount as a speeding car; and bacteria as much as a jet plane (Zotin 1978, 21–22).[7] Further, the flow of energies increases

---

[7] These figures do not take into account, as they should, the ratio

with the complexity of the organism: with very large variations within each group, cold-blooded multicellular organisms use eight times as much energy per gram weight as do unicellular organisms and warm-blooded ones 222 times as much (Zotin and Kanoplev 1978, 144). Internal organic processes still further multiply these energies. Davydov (1985, 3) hypothesizes that the energy generated by the hydrolysis of ATP, the energy unit in organisms, is transported by solitons along alpha-helix protein molecules without loss of energy.

Classical mechanics, with its equality of action and reaction, declared that energy could not multiply. No effect could be "greater than"—more complex or more powerful—than its cause. But synergies occur everywhere, and they are maintained when they arrange themselves in recursive loops. Thus, just as a soliton in the form of a tidal wave "passes through" the waves of the Pacific Ocean without altering them or losing its form and strength, so solitons carry "messages" through nerves or energy along muscles in the body. The solitons are energy at a higher level and with a unity of its own. They explain the tremendous energy produced in animals and plants from the much smaller amounts taken from their surroundings. The fact that birds in seasonal migrations can be shown on traditional theories not to be able to travel such long distances without stops is a *reductio ad absurdum* for classical theory.

At this point we can stop and note the importance of what we have been saying. We applauded Darwin for daring to believe what he saw: organisms maintaining themselves by competing with each other in an environment containing limited resources. Natural selection

---

between surface and volume of these objects.

was a competitive struggle. In the century and a half since then, during which we have studied extensively the way in which organisms maintain themselves, we have altered the picture in several important ways. We now see organisms as more complex systems and view their relationships, to their subsystems, other organisms, and their ecosystem, in an entirely different way. Cooperative or symbiotic relationships are at least as characteristic as competitive ones. Organisms depend upon elements of their ecosystem which enter into them but also affect the nature and dynamical stability of their ecosystem. Organisms couple with innumerable other systems, networking in such a way as to maintain their own looping processes. Synergies are achieved when systems organize themselves in ways which allow and sustain energy flows at higher levels. Everything is in process. Coevolution and coadjustment are everywhere. And the order which is displayed is produced by the dynamical systems which take these forms and enter into these relationships. It is produced from the bottom up, without planning, design, or purpose.

## 1.5   PHYSICAL THINGS AS DYNAMICAL SYSTEMS

Mainstream science has treated the physical and biological "realms" as different in kind. This has been bothersome from a theoretical point of view. Both physical and biological systems are real, and they interadjust. Reductionists have sought to explain biological facts in physical terms, but they have not succeeded. An adequate scientific theory should somehow explain their obvious interconnection. Varela proposed that organisms differ from nonliving things in being autopoietic. He has convinced us organisms are autopoietic, but he leaves us with a quandary. If organisms are organizationally open, as required by his theory, and can maintain their recursive processes at a higher level of energy flow only by coupling with surrounding systems, we have no possible explanation of their relationship with the nonliving elements in their environments unless the latter are also autopoietic processes that loop, couple, and fluctuate. "We cannot simultaneously hold that an organism is the smallest autopoietic unit and that organisms and environments are mutually determining." (Richard Lewontin in Tauber 1991, xvi) We can now resolve the difficulty. Physical events, as well as biological, are dynamical systems. Matter in all its forms is energy systems maintained at some distance from equilibrium by recursive processes.

Atoms are dynamic, i.e., energy in process, and systemic, i.e., organized as self-maintaining unities. They come into existence and maintain themselves in processes that are much like those found in living things. Matter is composed of atoms, as Newton believed, but they are not the simple, indivisible substances he thought they were. Atoms are constituted of recursive processes that maintain themselves and that are coupled with other systems having their own autopoietic needs. The organization and dynamism of atoms are well known. Positively charged protons and uncharged neutrons make up the nucleus of the atom. Together they comprise all but a few tenths of a percent of the mass of atoms and the universe. The negatively charged electrons are equal in number to the protons in the nucleus, but constitute only about 1/1800 its mass. The protons, tremendous by comparison with the electrons, create a terrific centripetal force, which the electrons can counteract only by orbiting about the nucleus at incredible speeds. Neutrons, protons, and electrons are all precariously poised masses fluctuating in a dynamically stable system; through their interadjustments, atoms are delicately balanced in their own dynamical stability.

Atoms autocatalyze and become autopoietic. The formation of matter is not different in kind from the formation of life. Each chemical element is created by a bombardment of energy upon neutrons at exceedingly high temperatures. The heavier the element, the higher the termperature, or energy, needed to form it and the rarer it is. The sun regularly converts hydrogen, the lightest atom, into helium, the next lightest, at about 20 million degrees Kelvin. Carbon, oxygen, and neon can be formed out of helium at temperatures about ten times that, at densities one thousand times greater than water. Elements with up to fourteen times the mass of helium (such as iron) can be formed at 4 to 5 billion degrees Kelvin. For elements heavier than this, the necessary temperatures can probably be found only in red giants and comparable stars (Cloud 1978, 12).

The orbital form adopted by atoms converts the extremely high and otherwise overwhelming energies to a recursive system of countervailing forces, which then maintains itself. Atoms couple by bonding in an electrochemical process in which electrons are shared or exchanged. Each atom is altered in the process through changes in its electrical charge, number of electrons, and relationships with other atoms. The elements are relatively stable systems of bonded atoms, and each of the elements is "arranged in a characteristic or systematically varying order" (12), which determines whether and how it can combine with other substances. Each element, in other words, is a dynamical system, autopoietic in its processes and interadjusting with coupled systems. What is possible for each element depends upon its atomic "structure," i.e., what atomic processes it has incorporated, and its surroundings, i.e., what systemic processes are available for coupling.

The formation and bonding of elements, in effect, extends the history of organic evolution to the physical elements out of which life was organized. "Elements, molecules, and other arrangements of atoms themselves have a history, even a kind of life-style. They grow and decay, depending on their surroundings, in a manner reminiscent of living things." And: "A kind of chemical selection played a key role in the evolution of the large organic but nonliving molecules from which the first living cells were made." (12, 146-47) This "evolutionary" chemistry was not only the same sort of catalytic process as that found in biological evolution, it was particularly predisposing to that later stage.

> There are excellent chemical reasons why hydro-gen, oxygen, nitrogen, and carbon and not four other elements are the key elemental building blocks of life. These are the four lightest elements that regularly exchange or share one, two, three, and four electrons. Hydrogen is the ideal energy broker in that it serves to move electrons, the basic energy source, from one site to another. Oxygen, nitrogen, and carbon are the only elements that regularly form double and triple chemical bonds with one another and with other elements. Because of this they make flexible structures of high chemical-bonding energy, good for build-ing cell walls, muscle fibers, and DNA.... Other

elements that are regularly involved in living organisms (such as phosphorus, calcium, and sulfur) also have special properties well suited to their functions—in energy exchange, for example. (146)

We tend to think of atoms and elements as fixed and stable, but they, like organisms, have a history which involved their catalyzation as self-maintaining systems at a higher energy level. They, too, must maintain that level of energy and can do so only by looping and coupling.

The networking familiar in organisms is also pervasive in nonliving things. They too depend upon couplings, perturbation-compensating fluctuations, and synergies to maintain themselves. Throughout nature, systems are formed by the pressure of energies too great to be absorbed by the existing systems; these then reorganize in the recursive—orbital, cyclical, spiral, helical, i.e., looping—forms which enable them to accept and multiply the energy. This is shown in the formation of more complex physical events: weather systems out of air currents, ocean currents, and planetary effects; solar systems out of matter distributed in space, etc.

A tornado is a simple physical example. It appears in certain weather systems which include high winds related in a certain way to each other and to the earth's rotation. These create an extreme difference in pressure between the center and edge of the storm. The winds then reorganize and multiply the energy of the system as they combine in a spiraling movement that balances and multiplies centripetal and centrifugal forces. The weather system and the gravitational effects of the earth combine to create the conditions for the tornado, but they do not cause it; the weather system creates turbulence so great a fork, or bifurcation point, is reached; the winds respond to the extremely high energies and the turbulence by forming the spiraling loops of a tornado. The energy of the new system multiplies and stabilizes, but it is a relatively fragile stability and does not last long.

Just because of its fragility, a tornado is a particularly good example of the formation of a natural system. It assumes a self-maintaining form not too dissimilar from the orbital stability of atoms, but it depends upon obtaining a steady supply of energy and materials from its surroundings to maintain its necessary but precarious balance between centripetal and centrifugal forces. Its history is that of mutually reinforcing events. Its energy increases as it catches materials in its swirl; the resultant increase in the power of its winds attracts more materials into its vortex, but the balance is delicate and easily upset. The elements, by contrast, are closer to equilibrium and easily maintain themselves in the earth's atmosphere.

All this means the line between living and nonliving events is blurred, for the instabilities built into the dynamical stabilities of autopoietic processes are contagious. Since some physical events are autopoietic, we must invert the usual accounts of the relationship of biological to physical events in nature. What we now find is that physical as well as biological events are accounted for better on the Darwinian model than the Newtonian one. With the exception of a few aggregates, such as rocks and sandpiles, physical events of all types and at all "levels" are autopoietic. The sun, for example, is a thermodynamic furnace in which nuclear reactions produce a nearly endless supply of energy that is radiated throughout the solar system. The energy it radiates is generated by its conversion of hydrogen atoms into helium atoms, and it is so great that the small share of its rays that strike the earth is sufficient to maintain the balance here, when it is combined with the energy of systems on earth. The biosphere is, in other words, an asymmetrical energy system maintaining its energy flows by preserving in its coupled processes the energy with which it is bombarded by the sun. It is Gaia, a dynamical, autopoietic system, but not an organism. Organisms are not different in kind from other events in nature, merely more complex. Both nonliving and living things are autopoietic energy systems. In all of them, systemic processes are dynamical. The mechanics of Newtonian physics has been replaced by an energetics. Nature is a dynamical system of dynamical systems.

## 1.6   The Nature of Nature

Nature is a network of networks. The dynamical systems model describes more accurately than does the control model what goes on in nature. In nature, control is not centralized and exercised by transmission from the top down in a hierarchical structure. In fact, it is not control but collaboration we observe in nature. Nature is made up of energy systems looping, coupling, and fluctuating in networks through which they share their resources to maintain themselves.

There are salient features of networking reality which deserve mention because they are so different from what classical scientific and metaphysical theories have told us to expect in nature.

First of all, natural events can be conceived as agents because each of them is actively maintaining itself by interadjusting with other agents and co-evolving with them and the networks they share.

Second, they do this by using their energies collaboratively. The more successfully they collaborate with other agents, the more successful their efforts to maintain themselves. Competition, paradoxically, is a form of collaboration.

Third, the collaboration takes the form of networking. Networking is characterized by causation which is reverberative in the sense that effects return upon their causes at a later stage of the latter's history.

Fourth, nothing is fixed or at equilibrium. Everything is always off-balance because what supports one agent's balance upsets the balance of others. Thus nothing is ever optimal for any agent or any network, but aways viable for all or most.

Fifth, networks created in this collaboration often display emergent qualities, that is to say, features which could not have been predicted on the basis of the qualities or activities of the agents.

Sixth, sometimes these emergent qualities involve synergies in which the power of both the network and the participating agents is sharply increased. The power of the network tends to be greater when the participating agents are numerous and/or differ from each other and therefore add to the variety of energies constituting the network.

Seventh, the farther systems are from equilibrium, the less linear are the reverberations they cause in the networks in which they participate. To some degree or other, effects are contingent.

This is how natural agents combine forces in networks. Our concern is, however, with human agents and the networks they create. Their networking will differ in quality from that found elsewhere in nature. Human experience is more complex because in human beings nervous systems have become self-conscious. Persons are themselves emergent features of nature. Using their feelings, desires, and intelligence, human beings establish relationships and direct their affairs on a new and more complicated basis. It is not simply life they maintain in their looping and coupling, their autopoietic activity, but the quality of their life. And they do this, not in accord with some set of instinctual responses, but through choices they make. These choices are, of course, conditioned by physical, biological, psychic, and social factors, and so are by no means "free." Still, they have a tremendous range.

What I want to do now is turn back to the aim I stated at the beginning. I want to find how we can best arrange our lives and relationships in order to improve as much as possible the quality of our lives. I shall begin by describing in the next chapter a new conception of what it means to be caring, one which has a strong resemblance to the kind of relationships found in networks. Following that I shall turn to recent theories of personality which, on the one hand, give ground to believe this description of caring is correct and, on the other, reveal healthy personality development as a networking process.

From the beginning the process will be revealed as both developmental and social—and in both respects ethical. In the course of exploring the implications— both personal and social—of caring, we shall find strong evidence that traditional ethics has adopted views of the good and the right which are based in outmoded views of nature and human nature. It will be our task to suggest the outlines of a new ethics, one which uses personal energies in ways that can be successful because people have feelings and intelligence and make decisions based upon them. They have the advantage that they can consider alternative routes, assess their progress, and learn from their experience. Within limits they can decide what kinds of networks to create and how to contribute to them.

That is what we decide when we adopt a philosophy of life. We are deciding who we are going to be and with whom and in what way we are going to share our lives and energies. The decision is a momentous one. I have described two models we can consider. One is highly regarded, but restricts networking; the other depends upon networking, which is now revealed as the way nature operates. Given our understanding of networking, we can expect that individuals will gain in individuality as they enter into supportive relationships with others. But what relationships have this quality? It is time to ask, What is the personal dynamic which best contributes to, strengthens, and benefits from the dynamism of networks?

# 2.

# The Personal Dynamic

October 1, 1998

THIS worldview, with its extensive supporting evidence from both nature and society, has implications for our image of ourselves. We are natural events, and so we must be dynamical unities. Our personhood consists in coalescing bio-psycho-social energies. Society and its institutions are networks created by our relationships with each other. Our "looping" and "coupling" is what we are, and we should not be surprised to find that we achieve our uniqueness by entering into supportive relationships and become more responsible socially by developing our individuality. But our "couplings" and "loopings" are not necessarily mutually supportive. In fact, it is obviously true, and a serious indictment of our society, that personal and social aims very frequently conflict with each other. When they do, both we as unique persons and the institutions through which we try to work together are weakened. It is only when and to the extent personal and social needs are in rough accord that synergies can appear. When they are, energies are multiplied and new unities achieved. Even then, though, we can only achieve our unique unity among others who are seeking theirs. Since theirs is often incompatible with ours, at least in detail, none of us will get everything we want, nor will any joint aim be satisfied perfectly.

We can't create utopia, but some arrangements are better than others. The whirlpool effect, the synergy, of the modernizing world was created as individuals, on the one hand, gained autonomy greater than they had experienced in earlier societies and, on the other, created institutions more responsive to their needs. What was it about these modern people which allowed them to be more decisive, less bound by tradition, more imaginative and adventurous, so that their newly designed institutions could gain this increased power? We have noted that even those who detected the increased power and connected it with the increased freedom could not explain the situation in dynamical terms. Having no theory of how things work which made their observations intelligible, they could only describe the effects produced. In spite of the remarkable changes, the control model continued to dominate western thought. In fact, advances were explained as the result of improvements in our ability to construct more powerful control systems. Technology was an outstanding feature of the modern world, and its creations were control systems; the successes of technology reinforced the control model. Consequently, scientific, social, and psychological analyses were hampered by continued reliance upon the control model, and only recently have they begun to break free. Now advances are being made in all these areas, and the most profitable theories are those which use the dynamical systems model.

We are interested in how ethical and social theory are affected by this new model. I begin at the very heart of things, by identifying the dynamic in personality which at the same time furthers our development as unique persons and strengthens our relationships with others. A motive which did this—that is to say, looped (aided personal development) and coupled (strengthened nurturing relationships) effectively—would create a strong network, that is, reveal order without control.

Such a motive would not be expected in classical ethical theory, which has been hobbled for centuries by descriptions of generosity, altruism, fellow-feeling, sympathy, and even love, as motives or feelings in which personal needs and desires must be set aside in favor of the needs of others. Influenced by this notion, we have come to think of personal fulfillment as the antithesis of concern for others. To be caring was to sacrifice what one really wanted in favor of what one "should" want. Ethical conduct required control of feelings thought to be based in human nature, and so alternative views were dismissed as romantic or sentimental. Thus it is only now, deep into the modernizing process which has uprooted and replaced so many of our traditional beliefs, that a revolutionary redescription of caring can be made, to reveal the dynamism in personality which helps us to achieve satisfying and worthwhile lives in nurturing communities.

## 2.1   Companionate Caring

It was Nel Noddings who first provided a phenomenology of caring which broke with classical accounts. Its pertinence for our project lies in the fact that she described caring as a complex of feelings, motives, and conduct which *affirms* another while *enriching* oneself.

She did not have it in mind to cause a revolution, although as a feminist she thought understanding of our relationships with each other was deficient. She simply wanted to offer a phenomenology of caring that remained close to the reality of an experience to which one can gain access only subjectively. She did that, but it was the experience of people in modern society, people who are accustomed to accepting others as unique in their capabilities and aspirations, sensitive to the need we all have for nurturing, and capable of responding sensitively to their own feelings, and those of others. It was, thus, at odds with traditional accounts of personal encounters to which the name had been given. Caring had been given a central place in moral and religious philosophies, but the values it supported were external to the caring experience Noddings described. Thus Noddings' description calls for an entirely different ethics, one based in the redescribed caring itself. What this means will become apparent only gradually. We must start with Noddings' account itself. In it we will recognize experiences we have had and treasured.

In "natural caring," she wrote, the "one-caring" and the "cared-for" *receive* each other. The caring person receives the feelings of the one cared-for, and the cared-for receives from the one-caring, not a gift or service, but the caring attitude itself. Thus caring is a "feeling with." (Noddings 1984, 5, 30) Noddings is radical in making receptivity a key element in caring. It has traditionally been thought a caring person gives rather than receives, and to reverse this view is to make a complete change.

The feeling the one-caring receives is the cared-for's feeling of need. For example, distress may be felt by the cared-for and communicated to the one-caring. The distress is then *felt by the one-caring*. The one-caring, in caring, sees through the eyes of the cared-for and feels, to the extent he[8] can, as the cared-for feels. The one-caring "becomes a duality": the seeing and feeling are his, but only partly and temporarily his, as on loan to him (30). The borrowed vision permits a shared feeling. This is possible only if the one-caring puts aside for the moment the habit of, or temptation to, make his own judgment of the "correctness," moral or political, of what the cared-for is doing or feeling. Thus caring is "largely reactive and responsive... receptive." (19) Receiving the other is an act of "inclusion"; the feelings of the cared-for become the feelings of the one-caring. Noddings calls this the *engrossment* of the one-caring in the cares and troubles of the cared-for. Engrossment is primarily a matter of feeling; it is nonrational (25) and comes before a judgment is made about the appropriateness or quality of the feeling received.

For the cared-for what is received is the caring *attitude* (59, 75), "an attitude that warms and comforts" him. (19) "The one cared-for sees the concern, delight, or interest in the eyes of the one-caring and feels her warmth." (19) When the cared-for recognizes that the one-caring cares for him, he "receives the caring honestly. He receives it: he does not hide from it or deny it." His reception of the

---

[8] For Noddings the one-caring is always referred to as a female and the cared-for as a male. She is protesting with good cause a tradition in which males are the protectors and females need protection, and her usage provides a useful reminder. I shall use different pronouns, not because I disagree with her, for I do not, but in order to protest the twin tradition, equally vicious, that portrays men as less capable of caring and commitment. My hope is that both stereotypes will be weakened.

one-caring is a feeling which focuses upon the particular nature of the one-caring's engrossment—worry, delight, relief—and responds specifically to that, affecting his motivation and behavior (69).

These feelings aroused in the cared-for by the caring attitude of the one-caring affect his motivation, which is enhanced. Noddings believes there is a natural desire to do well what one is doing, and she believes the caring relationship enhances both competence in one's tasks and this desire for "a global mastery of conditions in one's personal and professional environment." The cared-for is "encouraged to try by the acceptance" of the one-caring and "the natural effectance motivation is enhanced." He "'grows' and 'glows'", displays "buoyant responsiveness", willingly and unselfconsciously reveals himself, and "shares his aspirations, appraisals, and accomplishments" with the one-caring (62–73).

But even more important than the enhancement of motivation and the improvement of competence is the strengthening of the sense of self. A qualitative change occurs in the cared-for; he sees himself as worthwhile and is empowered to achieve his unique individuality. The cared-for "feels not so much that he has been given something as that something has been added to him." (20) He is freed, confirmed (67). He is enabled to re-examine his conduct and attitudes (59), accept greater challenges (64), be more open. Accepted as a person with weaknesses and problems, but also as a person showing promise, he is able to accept as a challenge what had been a threat. Since the one-caring supports him as a responsible person, the cared-for is free to decide for himself. Able to be himself more freely, he responds in a way that is uniquely his. He recognizes possibilities that are real for *him*, achieves the worth that *he* has, establishes the unique personhood that is *his*, and expresses himself in his own way. He acts more expressively and more spontaneously in his efforts to be himself. The "cared-for is free to respond as himself, to create, to follow his interests without unnecessary fear and anxiety" (72), to be free, creative, and spontaneous (74).

The one-caring is also changed dramatically, but perhaps less obviously. He is now motivated by the hopes and troubles of the object of his caring. If he cares deeply, he is affected as strongly by them as he is by those that arise out of his own needs and achievements. He is discovering himself as one whose concerns are not limited to his own needs and wants. He becomes involved in the lives of others and enters more directly and emotionally into the world around him. The boundaries—or barriers— between him and those around him are blurred, and he is more at home in his surroundings. He is a different person because he cares.

Caring is most effective when the one-caring receives many and varied feelings from the one cared-for. It is not just cares and troubles, frustrations and anxieties, that express needs. There is also need for appreciation, and the appropriate forms of caring may be praise, expressions of confidence, or evidence that the supportive person relies upon the one cared-for. These reactions also are confirmatory; they nurture the success they applaud. Indeed, since the confirmation given the cared-for allows him to act more adventurously and take greater risks in his efforts to gain fulfillment, it is important that he have the encouragement that comes with praise and support for his successful ventures. Caring is especially valuable and sweet when it shares moments of pleasure and success.

Sustained and mutual caring will include these as well as the feelings associated with hurt and failure.

This account reveals caring as a powerful bonding process in which both the one-caring and the one cared-for are strengthened and transformed. The bonding is that of two people who are struggling to fulfill themselves and who see each other in this light. The mutuality of their caring relationship sustains them in that effort, giving them the strength to clarify and act on their visions of the persons they can and want to become. The power generated by caring is the dynamic we are looking for in personal and social life. I shall refer to caring conceived in this fashion as *companionate caring* to distinguish it from the traditional analysis of caring. The designation highlights the fact that it cannot occur unless the two (or more) persons involved accept each other as capable of growth, in need of support, and responsive to nurturing support.

Since caring is the dynamic we can use to deal with the problem which seems so insoluble, namely, how we can strengthen the bonds between and among people while still encouraging personal autonomy and initiative, it is important that we get as clear and specific an idea of it as possible. I shall, therefore, go into greater detail, giving a closer analysis of companionate caring. I shall go beyond the description Noddings has made, but in a way I think consistent with her understanding of the experience. I shall represent companionate caring as a sequence of steps, but this is deceptive. Caring is a process, moving and seamless. An act of caring arises in a personal history: it focuses that history and reveals the person whose history it is. The personal history is a biography: To act in a caring fashion is to be a person who is caring. It is because caring is an expression of what is important to a person that it generates so much power. We need to note that before undertaking our analysis; otherwise, we may see caring as no more than a tactic for getting along in the world. As an expression of what a person gives high priority to, though, caring can occur only in the synergistic dynamics of personal arousal that it represents. With the understanding that caring is a seamless and generative flowing of feelings and motives for both the one caring and the one cherished, let us proceed with a description of an act of caring which, though artificially schematic and sequential, reveals its complexity and allows us to highlight the features which distinguish companionate caring from traditional caring.

We have said caring requires activity on the part of both the one who cares and the one who is cherished.[9] From the perspective of the one who cares

1. We are caring when we imaginatively intuit the situation of another

2. and experience as our own the feelings appropriate to it; reacting in this way,

---

[9] I introduce at this point a word that Noddings does not use in any technical sense in order to distinguish between the "natural" feeling and that same feeling in the context of motivational, affective, intentional, and behavioral elements it sets in motion. Noddings quite rightly points to the latter as the "completion" of the former, thus maintaining that they are inseparable psychologically. In spite of the fact that I agree with her in this, the word "caring" has been used in a variety of ways and contexts—as, for example, referring to health care, professional care—that permit misunderstandings to arise. By using the word "cherishing" to refer to the central, animating feeling, I attempt to avoid those misunderstandings.

3. we want to support the other in his efforts to deal with it,

4. but recognize that his feelings, which ours duplicate, are appropriate to the situation as he interprets it

5. and the responsibility for dealing with the situation is his; thus,

6. we communicate to him that we understand how he feels and care about him in his circumstances,

7. receive his appreciative acceptance of our caring,

8. and offer our support to him as and if he wishes it.

From the point of view of the one who is cherished

1. We feel cherished when we feel another person knows how we feel and

2. understands why we feel as we do

3. because he accepts us as we are

4. and appreciates our hopes and fears as indications of who we want to be;

5. we recognize that he cares,

6. and we accept and appreciate his caring and understanding

7. and are open to his encouragement and support as we find it helpful.

As this analytical summary makes clear, even the simplest act of caring is highly complex for both the people involved. It draws on emotional, motivational, intellectual, aesthetic, and, usually, physical resources, thus requiring us to draw together all our energies.

There are a number of features of companionate caring which mark it off from traditional accounts. In them, taken together, we can recognize a relationship we experience and consider highly important.

## 2.2  "Receiving" the Other

Caring begins as we receive the feelings of another. To do so caringly is to feel their impact as if they were our own, the product of events that have happened to us, but to recognize them as the feelings of the other, the natural result for him of what has happened to him.

We cannot have the feelings of another, and so we can receive his feelings only if we understand events from his point of view. The reception, therefore, is not in the least passive; it involves an imaginative construction of the other's circumstances, needs and wants, and self-image. In the simplest case, this is easy. We see a stranger peeling an apple; the knife slips and cuts his finger; the blood gushes, and he yelps and drops the knife. We know how he feels, and we can almost feel his pain. We have seen everything we need to see to interpret the situation and his reaction. We don't need to know more—why he was peeling the apple, whether he considers himself dexterous or clumsy, whether he heals quickly. But in most situations, interpretation is more difficult. We hear that a friend has won a second-place award. Is he elated at his success or devastated at loss of first place? Another has lost her father? Is she devastated by the loss or glad he died quickly and thus escaped a painful terminal illness? In each case, in any case, we need to know the facts that are relevant and this depends on how they are related to the expectations, anxieties, hopes, and aims of the one who is encountering them. They fit into his life; the circumstances become his situation as he interprets them, and his feelings respond to his situation rather than to the circumstances. We have, therefore, to be aware of his expectations, anxieties, hopes, and aims as well as his circumstances; only then can we construct his situation and intuit his feelings accurately.

We imaginatively construct another person, his situation and his feelings, but it is our construction, not his, and it affects us. Thus, to describe caring as originating in an act of receiving the feelings of another stands in contrast to the more common way of describing the experience. It is often said that in order to understand another we must put ourselves in his place, in his shoes. This is both true and false. It is true in that we must see the situation from his point of view if we are to intuit the feelings he has. But it is false if it implies, as it sometimes does, that we must set aside our own concerns in order to do this. We do not leave ourselves behind in order to enter into his experience; we are the ones making the inferences about what he is experiencing and having the feelings appropriate to that intuited situation. If we are correct in our intuitions, our inferences duplicate his and our understanding of his concerns is correct. We are aware of his concerns—and, because we care, they are ours, too.

We do not enter into his concerns at this stage; *he enters into our concerns*. We receive his feelings.

Noddings' revolutionary insight turns on its head what it means to care. The traditional accounts of caring—whether called caring, sympathy, empathy, fellow feeling, generosity, charity, love, or something else—describe us as moving away from ourselves, as dropping our own concerns in order to respond to the concerns of the other. Noddings, to the contrary, describes it as adopting the concern of another as a concern of our own. The imaginative construct is of another and his situation, of his feelings, but the feelings are now our own, also. The first step in caring is "receiving" another's feelings, not offering something to someone else. *Caring is emotionally a gain rather than a loss.*

In caring we are extending the range of what moves us, adding to the list of needs we must satisfy if we are to be happy. Importantly, we are developing concerns which lie beyond our own self-interests. In doing this we are refuting another profound misunderstanding, one which has implications for our notions of personality, right and wrong, and social ideals, namely, that caring involves a merging of the one caring and the one cherished. Sometimes this is merely a poetic way of speaking: it conveys the closeness that is felt in caring, what a psychologist calls "identifying with" a person or project or aim. But in other cases it clearly is intended to be taken literally. To take but one very influential example: Aquinas described one effect of love as "mutual indwelling," whether the love was of God or another human being. "Every love," he wrote, "makes the beloved to be in the lover, and vice versa." (Aquinas 1947, I-II, Q28, A2) But what we are describing is not a merger, but an imaginative bridging between autonomous beings. Our feelings and those of the one we cherish are not identical; they are duplicates.

We feel as he feels. But the feelings we have are ours. They are intuitive in their undeniable immediacy. We really think we know what is happening to the other, and what is happening really affects us, often with an irresistible emotional impact. But it is not a mystical experience. It is nothing more than an inference delicately based in sensitiveness to another's situation. It is an entirely natural, indeed, a normal and necessary feature, of our lives. It makes possible a close linking, but no merger.

The imaginative reconstruction makes the experience of another accessible to us, and thus makes possible an enlargement of our concerns and of the self we are. Like any growth, this requires change in us. Specifically, we must suspend our prior evaluations if we are to become more sensitive to the conditions the other is encountering and more responsive to his cares and troubles. We must set aside earlier estimates of what he is like, or judgments of what he should consider enjoyable, frustrating, or important. Any of these can interfere with our understanding of what he is experiencing. We want to know, with respect to all of these things, what *he* thinks and how *he* feels. In our current locution, we say we should not be "judgmental." The meaning is specific and limited. It does not call upon us to discard our own sense of what is true and good, either for us or the other; it certainly does not require us to forgo making the judgment we must make about how he approaches his circumstances and how he feels. It calls upon us merely to suspend any judgments which interfere with our ability to imagine what he is feeling and thinking. It means stepping aside, disengaging from other concerns, other commitments and loyalties, other strategies and programs, out of *this* concern. There is no diminution of self in so prioritizing our concerns. The concern is for an outcome in another's life, but the prioritization is exactly the same as that we make when the outcome is in our own life—when we decide whether to exercise or diet or be truthful or keep a promise. We are in either case deciding what is most important for us right here and now, what is of most concern to us. It is most important that our chief concern can be the condition of another.

It is feelings that are received in caring, and they may be of any sort whatever. They may arise out of failure, frustration, anxiety, hurt, doubt, or loss, and there the reception is certainly appropriate. But caring is also an appropriate response to success, glee, discovery, wonderment, generosity, pleasure, or joy. There our response may require no more than being present to share or applaud or praise or acknowledge the other, but these responses are also caring if they respond to the feelings of the one cherished. Our caring does not consist in responding to the need which, rightly or wrongly, arouses his feelings, but in responding to him because he has the feelings—and specifically in a way that is nurturing for him while they are present. He is capable of being nurtured because he has hopes and dreams, and hopes and dreams and lofty aims are as much a part of a person's being as are the blockages and deprivations he encounters in pursuing them.

## 2.3   Othering

I have been calling the cherished one an "other." The word has been used in many ways recently, and so I should make clear that I borrow the word from theologians, who make the experience of otherness a necessary aspect of spirituality. The most moving, most transformative, most meaningful experiences, they assert, grow out of our sensitivity and responsiveness to that which is not us and yet which is responsive to us and with which we must come to terms. For them this is a divine presence, but, whatever our religious views, we can see this relationship of otherness and potential spirituality in any caring relationship. The otherness of the other is always there and acknowledged by a caring person.

For this reason caring is a prime, and perhaps the prime, example of the sensitive-responsive nature of human beings. We cannot be sensitive without responding; we cannot respond unless we are sensitive. There is a dual quality to all human experience; neither aspect can exist without the other. In receiving the feelings of another, we feel them as our own but know they belong to the other. We cannot feel them unless, through an imaginative construction, we see the other as he sees himself, see his situation as he sees it, and therefore see the person he wants to be, the one whose feelings, of delight or frustration, are aroused by his situation. In other words, we cannot receive his feelings as ours unless we make an other of him and accept that other as he is, affirm him as the person he would be, and understand his feelings as appropriate.

But we are not, in making him an other, simply objectifying him, we are making him *our* other, one we cherish. He is not an object for us, but someone we care about. His feelings affect us as they affect him just because he is ours in the same way our bodies, our aims, and our situations, are ours. It is only because we accept him as an other that we can offer ourselves to him as his caring other. The other, being our "one cared-for," is unique. This is strange to say, but we can perhaps understand it if we think of a parent cherishing two children or a child cherishing his parents. We would never consider treating them exactly alike, not if we cared. Our caring permits us to see them as they are, as unique, having different strengths and weaknesses, sensitivities, frustrations, and delights. We respond to and appeal to our other as to no one else, even another whom we cherish. The response is specific and personal. It is what makes understandable our use of the word "cherish." To care is to respond to a particular, special person, for the concern must be the concern he has and this is unlike anyone else's. Every caring relationship rests in the displacement of one's motives to the particular concerns of a unique person. A caring person cherishes *this* person, experiences *his* particular situation as it is related to *his* real possibilities. No one cares for people selected randomly, and no one wants to be cherished by just anyone.

The "othering" that goes on in caring heightens the sensitivity and responsiveness of both the one caring and the one cared-for and therefore cultivates important personal qualities in each of them. Each is more fully him/herself, more uniquely individual, as s/he participates in the process of caring. The concerns of one we cherish become our concerns. Noddings calls this our "engrossment" in his "cares and troubles," and she describes it as a "motivational displacement." (Noddings 1984, 16) This calls attention, first of all, to the fact that the feelings we receive in caring motivate us. Our reaction is feelingful, and the feelings are so strong that they carry with them a desire, a motivation, an impulse to do something. The response is a feeling becoming a desire. A professional may be expert at analyzing needs and designing helpful programs, but he need not be caring. Caring requires that we feel *impelled* to do something out of our concern. The desire has the force of an imperative, "I must do something." The desire and motive are natural; they develop out of our own concern and result from the cultivation of our own sensitivities. The feeling of "I must" has a dual thrust. On the one hand it expresses our desire to respond to another; on the other, it expresses our desire to assert ourself. But the two are but two faces of the same imperative: to care is to *assert oneself* by *responding to another*. In caring, we are shaping ourselves as we find what we have to offer that is supportive of the other, that is, what he considers satisfying and worthwhile.

The othering essential to companionate caring must be distinguished sharply from other conceptions of the other. In many discussions of personality and personal relationships, the "other" is someone objectified, excluded, or exploited. Thus to accept another as other is, in effect, to reject or use him. But these inferences are made from premises that have been rejected by the dynamical approach. The self is not rigidly bounded and defending or asserting itself against what lies beyond it. The self is networking, completing itself in its relationships. Our tradition idealizes the use of power in exploiting the others of our experience. Most of these others are things, and so there is a temptation to treat people as things, also. We rightly fear this exploitative approach because it is so firmly established in our culture and so deeply embedded in our habits and thought processes, but it is not necessary, merely historically conditioned. It is the way we treat things and people in control systems; it is disruptive in the networking of dynamical systems. Whereas in power relationships we treat people as objects, as things to be used for our benefit, in caring relationships we treat them as persons, to be appreciated and supported and worked with. We can only care for others if they are others, but to be caring we must receive them as persons rather than use them as things.

The displacement of motives involved in caring is, then, part of the growth process of one who is caring. It is a way he finds out what is important to him. His caring expresses itself in the form of an imperative, and it is this which gives caring its dynamism.

## 2.4   Cherishing

We human beings, unlike other living things, find ourselves a problem. We don't instinctively know what we want, and so our problem is to shape as well as to satisfy our desires. This, however, is a never-ending process. We can always find new and better ways to satisfy our desires, and we can always find that satisfying them is not enough. When the latter happens, we are, whether we know it or not, outgrowing our concerns. We can only satisfy ourselves by finding new things to enjoy and worry about. This improves the quality of our lives, and it is going on all the time. We human beings are never completed. We are developing. Thus it remains always a question of signal importance: What can I, what should I, make of myself? Our most important concerns deal with this, the problem of the self. In caring we see others also as problems to themselves. We receive them, and we receive them as others, but we also communicate to them our feelings about what we have received from them as our cherished other. To do this is to cherish them. What does it mean to cherish another: What do we communicate to another that constitutes cherishing him?

First of all, we communicate that we care. The message is the simplest possible, perhaps only "Oh, no!" or "Wow!" or "How wonderful!" or "How terrible!" We let the cherished one know "we recognize the spot you are in"; "we see what troubles or elates you"; "we care"; "we are here." All of these are part of our initial message, which may, of course, be by glance or hug or pat on the arm rather than in words. The details of the message, the way it is delivered, even whether it is delivered, depends upon our sense of what the one we cherish needs, what we have to offer, and how he may receive us. We place ourselves at his side.

Second, we *accept* him. This has already been implied in our picture of the task of imaginative construction we found prerequisite to receiving his feelings. There we were noting that we could not convince him that we understood his plight, his cares and troubles, unless we reflected them back to him accurately. Here we make a closely related point: we care because we appreciate him as he is and with his cares and troubles. *Because he is the person he is*, he is challenged, frustrated, or pleased by the circumstances he finds himself in. *Because he is the person he is*, we see the growth possibilities and therefore understand both why he feels and acts as he does and why that is or is not satisfying for him. Our acceptance is highly personal. We may know in the abstract that all reactions make some sense from the point of view of the person involved, but we are reacting to one whose frustration or joy is ours, too. We see why his reaction makes sense to him and care enough about him to accept him as the person for whom this reaction is sensible or required. Our acceptance is specific and personal.

To accept him as he is and with his reaction does not require, though, that we approve his actions. We may, in fact, disapprove heartily. Suppose the one we cherish is an alcoholic, is caught cheating, ignores traffic tickets, or gambles away needed household funds and we disapprove. We cannot pretend we approve and we cannot ignore the ethical issues. We could, of course, give up on such a person, but what if we care? What, in fact, does it mean to continue to care in such circumstances? It means no less than that we continue to think this person has worth and is capable of realizing it; that is to say, he is sensitive and responsive and may still mobilize his resources to achieve a satisfying and worthwhile life. What support we will provide him depends in part upon what the failure is that we do not condone, in part upon what we think his real possibilities are at this juncture, and in part what we have to offer him, given our own limitations and the relationship we have with him. These are questions to be dealt with later, but they do not arise unless we accept him as he is and with his cares and troubles and make this clear to him.

Having accepted our cherished one, we can go on, third, to *affirm* him. What we affirm is the worth that he can achieve and to which he aspires. The worth is his and only his, and so affirming him, like accepting him, is a response to him as a person. But now it is seeing him as the person he can be and wants to be. That prospective view is important. The frustrations or successes that aroused his feelings, and ours, in the first place are such just because the events occur in the context of his hopes and fears. They have the meaning they have because he has the hopes he has. In cherishing him we live his hopes. We encourage him in these hopes by seeing him, not only as he is, but also as he is trying to be. Our caring vision is bifocal: we accept him as he is and affirm him as the person he wants to become.

Acceptance and affirmation, combined, constitute understanding, but understanding is not simply an intellectual exercise. To *have* understanding of another is to recognize how he views himself and his circumstances, to know what he would like to make of himself and what he thinks the prospects of doing that are. It is a kind of knowing. To *be* understanding is to accept him as he is, affirm him as he wishes or hopes or might be, and to feel the "I must." It is a kind of being. Each act of caring requires motivational displacement, the internalization of concern. It is this understanding which can be felt by the one cherished. Receiving the feelings and attitudes contained in it, he is opened to caring and the nurturing support it offers.

## 2.5   Being Cherished

The cherished one's needs and hopes breed cares and troubles as he confronts his circumstances with his expectations. His feelings are aroused, and these open him to caring. The situation may be problematic or consummatory; in either case he is moved. In one respect life is like a game of Trip to Jerusalem. Success or failure requires movement and entails risks. We are always on the move, trying to satisfy our needs and hopes, and so we are always vulnerable. The threat may be to what we are doing, in which case the support may be simply technical, as when a colleague writes a letter of recommendation or an instructor offers advice or a friend helps us repair our car. But the more important threats are those which call in question our values, aims, and hopes; then we need nurturing.

That is when we most need to feel cherished. When we are vulnerable, our feelings are surging through us. If the situation is particularly poignant, devastating, exhilarating, or momentous, we may be swamped by them. We are at our most sensitive and only too ready to be defensive, to turn away from others, whom we may regard as sources of danger because they don't "understand" us. The slightest sign that one who claims to care does not understand and accept us creates a barrier between us. This can happen in a number of ways. Our would-be carer may have incorrectly interpreted our situation. Or he may have failed to see how we view ourselves, our competence, our problems, or progress. Or he may have misunderstood our hopes for ourselves, our anxieties, or our values. If he errs on any of these counts, he will misunderstand us, fail to perceive our feelings, and therefore find his "I must" misdirected. His caring will not be "completed" in the one cherished.

If, however, he avoids all these pitfalls, the rewards are great, for then his elation, sympathy, hurt, frustration, or whatever, mirror our own. His reaction confirms us in our own and thus reinforces our hopes and aims, increases our resolve, validates our frustration, objectifies our hurt. We see that our feelings, no matter how overwhelming they may be in their initial impact, are understandable to a sensitive person concerned for our well-being. We are understood and accepted, and this encourages and strengthens us. In the extreme, our feelings have been aroused because we are encountering problems that seem insoluble or find ourselves in circumstances with which we feel unqualified to deal. We have begun to doubt ourselves, to question whether we can manage this loss or deal with these odds. In other words, we are having trouble accepting ourselves. Now along comes someone who, appraising our situation as we do, thinks we are up to it. We are, all of sudden, better able to see ourselves as strong, competent, experienced, able to deal with the threat. The emotional release is intensified because it is shared, but at the same time the energy released by the emotions becomes more manageable. We are no longer isolated and doubtful, for someone who cares thinks our feelings are appropriate. We find it easier to believe we are competent and worthwhile, for someone has recognized our hopes and expectations. We have someone to turn to. We may for the moment relax in the understanding of the caring other. It is only when we have reached this moment that we are open to nurturing support. Before this we may have been able to accept help, but now we can allow ourselves to be nurtured. We turn from our feelings to the situation that engendered them. Sustained by the understanding of a caring other, we can focus upon what needs to be done with one who cherishes us alongside.


## 2.6   Nurturing

It is only at this stage, when these exchanges have taken place and these feelings have been shared, that we can offer support to the one we cherish. We can offer support and it can be accepted because a bond has been created between us. We have developed an understanding, shared hopes and dreams, confronted obstacles together, and shared appropriate feelings. We stand arm-in-arm. We stand with the one we cherish. Our caring is companionate.

The impulse we have in caring is to nurture the one we cherish. This response is a uniquely human one, because it is only human beings who have what I have called the problem of the self. Human beings are capable of becoming any of many different selves, and they must choose which one they will be. Nurturing consists in cultivating the specific hopes and expectations of the one we cherish, by helping him to deal with the specific difficulties and successes made important for him by those hopes and expectations. In companionate caring, the desired change is developmental rather than corrective. The development can only take place *in* the one we cherish, and it can only represent *his* development when he makes the required decisions and takes the required steps. We can only stand ready to support and, if necessary, to attempt to persuade. We are colleagues rather than tutors. Nurturing is a relationship among moral equals.

Our caring stance is:

- "You are in charge—and I believe in you,"

- "You can do it—and I am here if I can help,"

- "You are the one to be commended, or who must deal with the mess, or who must shape up—and I am with you, to assist if I can, as you do."

Note that we make an offer, not a gift. We treat our cherished other as autonomous, competent, concerned, responsible, worthy. We do not intervene; we support.

We do not do what we think ought to be done for or by the other; we expect the other to do what he thinks best. We may or may not know what he should do, but we ask the question, Can I help you? In this way we respectfully acknowledge that he must rely upon himself. Our caring offers comfort, understanding, and nurturing, but it also offers a challenge and assistance. Because we receive our other as hurt but self-reliant, frustrated but responsible, a problem-solver with a serious problem, we encourage him to be a competent and reflective person. To offer support is not to offer escape, but encouragement. The supportive response is not to impose upon him what we think best, but to offer assistance to him as he tries to work out what he thinks best. We intervene when he indicates he wishes it. If we do not wait for that assent, we risk demeaning him. Suppose, for example, he loses his job and we "solve" his problem by offering him another. He may well think we are treating him as a "charity case" because we consider him incompetent. Or suppose he wants desperately to pass a test and we shade the standard in order to "help" him. We have responded to his anxiety but not his hopes. Or suppose he finds a new friend and we tell him truthfully of that person's very serious shortcomings. He may well think we don't trust him to arrive at the correct assessment himself. Notice that some of these responses may be the "correct" form of support once he has indicated his readiness to accept them. The difficulty is not that they are not needed, but that they have been offered before he has recognized they are needed. They have been offered gratuitously, and thus directively rather than supportively.

We have substituted our judgment for his, but he is the person who must use the situation to develop himself by cultivating his sensitivities, judgment, responsiveness, and sense of responsibility. It is his life that is being lived and his character that is being tested. The very fact that he can use support means that he is being sorely tested. He must develop a capability that he has not demonstrated previously, and that is something only he can do. We can assist only by helping him to gain or regain his vision of who he can and wants to be or by encouraging him to be that person.

Companionate caring is superior to traditional conceptions of caring just because, instead of doing something for someone else or directing him in overcoming his difficulties, we offer him support in his efforts to decide what he must do and how he can do it. Nurturing cultivates responsibility and self-reliance. We can encourage him by offering our understanding and support for his efforts. We can comfort him when he fails and share his delight when he succeeds. But we can't cut a path for him; our position is at his side. There we can be sensitive to his sense of his worth and assist him as he cultivates the responsibilities entailed in it. Companionate caring leaves the final decision to the cherished one, thus communicating to him that he is capable, responsible, and worthwhile.

## 2.7  The Synergies of Caring

Nel Noddings was interested principally in analyzing the least complex instance of caring, that between two people. Describing it with such sensitivity and astuteness was a great service. That meant, however, that the cumulative aspect of caring was left to be explored by others. The phenomenology she offered did not provide a basis for finding out either what happens when caring becomes general in society or what happens when a person's caring becomes habitual and characterizes his general attitude. We can say that the latter becomes a *concerned* person and the former becomes a *community*. It is when we have a community of concerned people that we can expect the effects of caring to become cumulative. The community becomes a network and relationships generally become caring. It is at this point that synergies can become common. This would be the natural outcome of looping and coupling which succeeds in strengthening participating systems and the bonds between them.

That is what happens in companionate caring. The autopoietic paradox is evident even in the relationships between two people. In companionate caring all those involved are able to overcome difficulties better and achieve greater satisfactions, not at the expense of others, but by nurturing them and being nurtured by them. Their relationships become closer and stronger in this way as they become more autonomous, competent, and confident. The dynamic unity, the personhood, of the participants, becomes more effective, as does the bond between them. The process is generative. Those who care and are cherished become more responsible. Caring is habit-forming and character building.

Contrast this with the way things happen when people are uncaring. They act in their own interest, but counter to the interests of others. What pleases one frustrates others. Hostilities may be aroused, which makes for unpleasantness. But even if they are not, everyone must "look out for himself." Each realizes others may see how they can gain at his expense, and so it becomes reasonable to be suspicious of everyone.

One does not find pleasure in the success of others, for one is only interested in what happens to himself, nor can one expect sympathy from others, for they are working on their own projects. Cooperation may exist, but it is limited: each is joining in only to benefit himself. Relationships last as long as they are advantageous. Smiles are false. Feelings are stunted and blunted. No one is entirely at ease with others, and feelings of isolation are common.

Live this way long enough, adopt a view of personality which claims this is the way people are by nature, develop a theory of reality which describes all relationships as external, and create institutions which reward competitive success, and this will seem entirely natural, indeed, inevitable. People will appeal to others on the basis of their self-interest. Trust will be the exception. People will take pride in their self-sufficiency, their "realistic" approach to life, their independence. They will throw themselves into educational and training programs for themselves and look down upon those who "fall behind" or "can't make it." We can recognize such a society; it is our own. Its synergies are weak. Each individual is acting strenuously to maintain himself but avoiding nurturing relationships with others. He is "looping" furiously but "coupling" only weakly.

We can distinguish such a society from a caring community by saying its members are self-interested while those participating in a caring community are concerned. The distinction is an important one. Interests are bounded by the advantage of the interested person; concerns include self-interests but go beyond them to include those which originate in the motivational displacement essential to caring and culminate in the nurturing of others. People are not "by nature" self-interested. They are concerned. If—or, rather, to the extent that—their society is a community of concern, they are not aloof from others, suspicious of them. They approach others in wonderment, wanting to find in what their unique worth consists.

The way in which caring concern creates and affects communities has yet to be explored, but even in person-to-person relationships we see how their collaborative and cumulative effects create synergies. In a caring person every act of caring activates, directs, sharpens, and develops the concern out of which it grows. Every concern heightens the sensitivities and responsiveness required in caring. The disposition and the reaction create a feed-forward loop in which each is strengthened and rewarded. The concern is not the same after it has been activated in caring; the caring is not the same after it has been put in play, exercised, refined, and made habitual. The process is one that feeds on itself. Our concerns express what we consider to be important, and therefore what is powered by our strongest feelings. We "have" our concerns because we have decided what is reasonable, important, and worthwhile. We have our values, priorities, and necessities, and our feelings are aroused when they are endangered or when we take significant steps toward realizing them. Our feelings stir us to action—give us energy to pursue our goals more forcefully.

Even on the basis of this preliminary analysis, limited to two people, we can see that caring is a process which feeds upon itself, thus creating synergies within and among people. Caring constitutes a feed-forward cycle which multiplies and directs energies in both those who care and those they cherish. Companionate caring energizes those who enter into it because of the mutualities it creates. Those who are caring and cherished nurture each other, thus encouraging each to be creative, confident—to be him/herself. Empowered in this way, each is able to be more nurturing. A network is set up in which personal development and nurturing relationships are married. What happens in each person, the one who cares and the one who is cherished, contributes both to his own development and satisfaction with life and the development and sense of satisfaction of the other.

## 2.8    THE CLASSICAL MODEL

This could not even be imagined until such synergies had become evident in the modernizing western world, where horizons are ever expanding and we have developed democratic political arrangements and pluralistic societies. In this setting Noddings' redescription of what it means to be caring is so natural we must ask why it is so revolutionary. The answer is simply that it runs counter to the received wisdom, which is supported by the worldview we have inherited from the classical world. I call this the classical model. It contains a theory of personality, a moral theory, a social theory, a theory of the family, and a metaphysical theory. These are all of a piece, constructions which use the control model.

Of all those who contributed to this construction Plato was the most important. It was he who first developed a systematic account of these topics, and later accounts, at least until very recently, were all variations on his theories. As Alfred North Whitehead once wrote, western intellectual history is a series of footnotes to Plato. When the Christian church fathers sought theoretical justification for their faith, they turned to Plato and Aristotle, Plato's student. As a result, religious and secular thinking combined to enforce the control model on western thinking, and we have thought that to explain order in any form we had to identify the rational plan by which it is brought into being and maintained.

Plato, as we shall see, had theories in many fields, but the key to his thinking lies in his ethical theory and the theory of personality he developed to support it. Plato was a student of Socrates, whose concern was only with ethics, and his early dialogues dealt with the issues Socrates framed: What does it mean to be good? What resources do we have available as we seek to be good? What makes it difficult to be good? And, like Noddings, he considered central the question, What part do feelings play in our efforts to be good? We have seen how Noddings answered this last question. Plato took an almost diametrically opposed position in answering it. This had tremendous implications for ethics, as we shall see.

Like his teacher Socrates, Plato gave priority to two virtues, *sophia* and *sophrosyne*. The former is wisdom, which Plato thought could be gained by contemplating eternal and unchanging Forms. The latter had several meanings and is harder to translate. For Plato it was self-control, a way of dealing with oneself, but it also referred to a personal quality, usually translated as moderation or temperance, and the mental state which made it possible, usually translated as sound-mindedness. It was only by acting with self-control because one was a temperate, self-disciplined person, Plato held, that one could be ethical.

*Sophrosyne* was closely related to *sophia*. Self-control was possible if one had wisdom, which involved the discovery of eternal truths, such as what is good. Self-control was the application of these eternal truths to the practical situations one encounters. This may sound excessively intellectualistic, and it was, as becomes clearer when we ask what it was Plato thought threatened moral conduct. The threat was posed by passions, pleasures, desires, appetites, fears, all of which had a tendency to become excessive and overpowering. If we were to choose one word to describe the danger it would be "feelings." Plato thought feelings inevitably tended to obstruct and weaken reason, the means by which we can discover what is true and good. To be ethical one must use reason to control and curb feelings.

This is the position Plato took throughout his dialogues. In the *Gorgias* he wrote, "Every man is his own ruler," and when asked what this meant, he said it consists in "being self-controlled, master of himself, ruling the pleasures and appetites within him." (491D) Later, in the *Republic*, he asserted "*sophrosyne* is a certain orderliness and mastery over certain pleasures and appetites." (430E) He saw life as a struggle between reason and passions. Plato distinguished between those who believe "it is not intelligence which governs [people]... but some other thing, at one time passion, at another pleasure, at another pain, sometimes love, and often fear" and those who believe "intelligence to be a noble thing, well-fitted to govern mankind." (*Protagoras* 352C) *Feelings were to be feared as the source of immorality*. Reason was the source of the control necessary to a well-ordered life.

Against the tradition based in this Platonic approach,

we can see at once the revolutionary impact of Noddings' description of what it means to be caring. For her, understanding begins in receiving feelings, and feelings are indicators of the hopes and frustrations we experience. Her position was exactly contrary to that of established western thinking, which had adopted Plato's ethics and social theory. She was radical because she was pointing out the falsity of what was perhaps the central tenet of classical theory, that ethical conduct requires the control and curbing of feelings, which interfere with understanding. Noddings was building upon nearly a century of investigation into the place of feelings in personality, investigation which led to the position that feelings must be integrated into personality if health, competence, and happiness are to be achieved. That position is now well-established, and Noddings' position seems the only rational one. It is important, therefore, to note that classical theory took the opposite direction.

Once he had explained immorality as defeat in a struggle against forces existing within oneself, Plato found himself forced to take the position that personality is divided. Since reason and passions are both in the self and yet opposed to each other, there must be at least two parts to the self. He finally decided it had three parts: a rational part, a spirited element, and base passions. The spirited element could be harnessed readily by reason, but virtue was to be achieved only by subduing ever-recalcitrant base passions. As Plato wrote about self-control:

> The expression seems to want to indicate that in
> the soul of the man himself there is a better part
> and a worse part; whenever what is by nature
> the better part is in control of the worse, this is

expressed by saying that a man is self-controlled or master of himself, and this is a term of praise. When, on the other hand, the smaller and better part, because of poor upbringing or bad company, is overpowered by the larger and worse, this is made a reproach and called being defeated by oneself, and a man in this condition is called uncontrolled. (*Republic* 431A–431B)

For Plato the good life could be achieved only if reason subjugated strong but "base" feelings and rejected the temptations they offered.

The theory of a divided self could not have been made clearer. "The soul and body are two." (Plato *Gorgias* 464B) By itself the *psyche* is perfect and perfectly wise, but it is "contaminated" by the body (Plato *Phaedo* 66B), so that it has trouble apprehending the truth. The body is, of course, what possesses passions and seeks pleasures, thus making it difficult for us to be virtuous. "The body fills us with passions and desires and fears, and all sorts of fancies and foolishness so that... it really makes it impossible for us to think at all." (66C) The soul is "compelled to regard realities through the body as through prison bars." (82E) Truth, which is first of all knowledge of what is good, "is in fact a purification from all these things [pleasures and pains and fears], and self-restraint and justice and courage and wisdom itself are a kind of purification" (69BC) such as mystics experience (69D). "Those who truly love wisdom refrain from all bodily desires and resist them firmly." (82C) Only in this renunciation can we "gain peace from these emotions." (64E) We are not to reform the world, Plato held, but to renounce it; not to integrate our feelings into our lives, but to overcome them.

If the body gains control, we are ruled by pleasures, which is called self-indulgence (69A). The only counter to that is self-control, which "consists in not being excited by the passions." (68C) This is, of course, where the need for ruling arises. "When the body and soul are joined together, nature directs the one to serve and be ruled, and the other to rule and be master." (80A) Thus self-control was a form of rule. Personality was a hierarchy; control was from the top down and essential. Just as one could not be strong without physical exercise, so also one could not be self-disciplined and wise "if he has not fought triumphantly against many pleasures and desires." (Plato *Laws* 647D) "In private each is an enemy of himself." (626D) Of all the victories it is possible to win, "the first and best" is the victory "of oneself over oneself," whereas "being defeated by oneself is the most shameful and at the same time the worst of all defeats." (626E) This theory of a divided self entered into the mainstream of western culture, where over the centuries the split became even more pronounced. In the classical period, the desires and pleasures were to be ruled, controlled, disciplined; when the tradition was Christianized, the project became more ambitious. Desires and pleasures were to be rooted out, extirpated, renounced. The divided self became one in which the parts could not be reconciled, and the struggle became one to the death. Over the centuries there have been great differences in the way the divided self has been viewed, but variations in details have been unimportant compared with the notion that a divided self is the only one imaginable.

A person divided against himself could not be more unlike a person caring companionately. The latter is acting upon his own concerns and in a supportive relationship with others, is entering into synergies, both in his own person and in his relationships with others. Energies are flowing freely and gaining strength. The former is fighting himself at every step of the way, directing his efforts at weakening his own feelings, denying himself pleasures, and seeking control over an enemy whose power is his own. The former is seeking fulfillment; the latter is practicing self-denial. It is easy to see Plato's legacy in our common belief that we must choose between personal satisfactions and worthwhile activities.

Plato's social theory developed the same themes as it brought the control model into social relationships. In them as in personal life control was necessary, but the discipline was to be exerted over others. The self-disciplined man, being moderate, was also wise and just, and so was justified in exercising power over others. For those incapable of such moderation, the proper solution was to "be enslaved to the best man, who has a divine ruler within himself." (Plato *Republic* 590C) In the household, each had his or her own place, but all of them, wife, children, and slaves, were properly under the control of the male head of household; his self-control legitimated his authority, and the others benefited from his direction.

Society also consisted of parts just as did the self, only now the parts were persons. These differed in their abilities and functions but could be brought into a harmonious arrangement if those who were guided by pleasures, desires, fears, etc., could be brought under the control of those who, being wise, knew what was right. "The great mass of multifarious appetites and pleasures and pains will be found to occur chiefly in children and women and slaves and, among those called free men, in the inferior multitude." Plato considered the ideal arrangement to be one in which "the desires of the inferior multitude will be controlled by the desires and wisdom of the superior few." (431B–431D) The rulers were comparable to the reasoning part of the self, the multitude to the base desires. In the state the wise ruler promulgated just laws for citizens who were incapable of self-discipline and so needed his guidance. Aristotle concurred. The ruler "ought to have moral virtue in perfection"; the ruled need only to have "that measure of virtue which is proper to each of them." (Aristotle *Politics* 1260A)

Justice would prevail in the city-state just as morality would in personal life, that is, when recalcitrant elements acceded to control by those which or who should rule. Just as a person is "temperate by reason of the unanimity and concord of all three [parts of the self], when there is no internal conflict between the ruling element and its two subjects, but all are agreed that reason should be ruler," (Plato *Republic* 442D) so also, "in our [ideal] state... the governors and the governed will share the same conviction on the question who ought to rule." (431DE) That state is just in which everyone contentedly performs tasks assigned to him by the wise and good.

Thus persons, families, and states were all conceived to be control systems with hierarchical structure and acceptance of controls imposed from the top. But Plato went even further: the universe was ordered, a cosmos, because it was structured in the same way. Thus Plato asserted that "partnership and friendship, orderliness, self-control, and justice hold together heaven and earth and gods and men, and that is why they call the universe a cosmos or world order, my friend, and not an undisciplined world-disorder." (*Gorgias* 508A) The cosmos, what we call nature, was for Plato a control system; his metaphysics used the control model. Order was introduced by a force or agency outside the system, which without that injection would be "chance effects without order or design." (*Timaeus* 46E)

By using the same model to describe and prescribe what is proper for everything from human beings to nature Plato created a worldview. The world is disciplined, and that is why we should be. We have a place in the universe, a role to play, and we must submit to the governance of the universe. In being good, we are performing the duties entailed by the role we are assigned in an ordered cosmos. Alasdair MacIntyre has recently claimed, probably correctly, that this was the view belonging to the Greek tradition antedating Plato, as well as being Plato's own. MacIntyre claimed that for Homer

> to conduct one's actions and affairs in accordance with ... an order structuring both nature and society.... [Specifically,] the order over which Zeus and human beings reign is one structured in terms of hierarchically ordered social rules. To know what is required of you is to know what your place is within that structure and to do what your role requires. (MacIntyre 1988, 14)

Illustrating the hold this view still has on us, MacIntyre approves it as one we should still accept.

As a worldview, Platonism was highly persuasive. It claimed to be rational and demand rationality, but it was a particular kind of rationality it used and promoted: linear thinking. There could only be one correct answer to any particular question; therefore, there could only be one good. In society that was the common good, which had the special merit that within it all personal values could be harmonized. Since what was good for society was also good for each citizen, individuals lost nothing by subordinating their own aims to the common good. In fact, they could achieve their own virtue only by obeying laws promulgated by the wise ruler, laws which, if obeyed, would guide the society toward its common good. Citizens had different roles to play in society, and it was their duty to perform the duties associated with those roles. Similarly, in the family, women, children, and slaves could be virtuous only by performing the duties assigned them by the male head of the household.

Plato did not have much to say about the kind of personal relationships Noddings described. This is perhaps not surprising, since it should be apparent by now that Noddings thinks what I have called companionate caring should be the pattern and matrix for healthy social arrangements while Plato considered justice, the "social virtue," to require an authoritarian social arrangement. Plato also discussed personal relationships, but not very clearly. He discussed friendship in the *Lysis*, but the dialogue has been called a failure and certainly it is not at all clear. It is important to understand, though, what ideal personal relationships are thought to be in a theory which postulates one good in a society arranged hierarchically specifically to achieve it. The clearest exposition of the topic is to be found in Aristotle's discussion of friendship in Books VIII and IX of his *Nicomachean Ethics*.

This became the standard account of how we should deal with one another. It is still highly respected, and it constitutes the original of the account of caring which was superseded by Noddings' phenomenology. Aristotle was describing a relationship he thought should hold between parents and children, among comrades (whom he believed to be more common among men than among women), and among fellow citizens. Friends, he wrote, guard and preserve prosperity, are a refuge in poverty and other misfortunes, keep the young from evil, minister to the needs of the elderly, and stimulate those in the prime of life to noble actions. "With friends men are more able both to think and to act." (Aristotle *Nicomachean Ethics* 1155a10-16) Friendship is more important even than justice, for friends have no need of justice whereas just people need friends. In fact, friendship is essential, "for without friends no one would choose to live." Friends are "objects of love," and objects are lovable, Aristotle asserted, only if they are good, pleasant, or useful, or at least seem to be so; so there are three kinds of friends, those bound by their shared pleasures, their usefulness to each other, or their shared virtue. And these fall into two classes. Those who love each other either for the sake of utility or pleasure love for the sake of what is good (useful or pleasant) for themselves. These friendships are "incidental"; they last as long as they are mutually useful or pleasant, and no longer.

There is a great gulf between these relationships and the third type, which Aristotle called "perfect friendship," and which he considered ideal. Perfect friendship is a relationship between good or virtuous people: they wish well to each other and they are themselves good (1156b7-9). Perfect friendship is superior because it exhibits virtue, which is the quality of those who, properly subjugating their feelings, pursue the good. Such friends are "alike in virtue." A perfect friend wishes the *good* for his friend. While this seems on its face to be acceptable, for surely friends wish the well-being of their friends, Aristotle meant something more and quite specific. The good a friend offers is what is good in general or, since he is virtuous and therefore knows what is good, good from his own point of view. A good friend, in other words, does not need to ask what his friend wants or thinks best; he is virtuous and therefore knows what the common good is. Knowing this, he knows how his friend fits into society and therefore what his duty is. He does what he as a friend knows to be good for his friend. Aristotle made the point in a second way, as if to underline its importance. He held that in friendships based upon mutual usefulness rather than mutual virtue, the utility is increased when the friends *differ* from one another so that each can be useful in his own way. The total of usefulness is increased in this way. But in friendships based in mutual virtue, friends must be *alike* in virtue. What he meant was that they must agree about what is good. The bond of friendship could hold only within the circle of moral agreement. In other words, friends offer "beneficence" to those who, agreeing with them about what is good, "need help." They offer charity rather than support. Neither the one caring nor the object of charity is unique; both the one offering help and the one receiving it are fungible. The relationship is scarcely personal at all.

This classical view of supportive personal relationships could not be more different from that offered by Noddings. Though Aristotle insisted there should be mutuality in friendship, he allowed no place for receiving the feelings of another; feelings were dangerously opposed to reason. He allowed no place for othering; neither autonomy nor responsibility were cultivated in friendship. Nor was nurturing elicited or valued; the relationship did not facilitate personal development, but encouraged conformity to rules originating elsewhere or, absent that, intervention to enforce conformity. Aristotle borrowed Plato's theory of a common good in which all other goods fit nicely and used it as a Procrustean bed to idealize subjugation to authority rather than the nurturing of unique persons.

The virtue promoted by this classical tradition is charity, which is expressed by doing *for* another what is *good* for him. We can call this the nanny theory of caring. Nannies supervise, direct, help, admonish, correct. Knowing what is right, they teach their charges what is right and how they should go about doing it. Knowing what is wrong, they teach their charges how to detect it in themselves, how to avoid it, how to feel guilty, and sometimes, unfortunately, how to dissemble. In other words, they pass on the common good, what others have taught them is right and good, asking only that their charges accept it without question. In order to do this, which requires that personal needs and wants be set aside, they divide the selves of their charges into a virtuous, obedient part and an emotional, willful one. Generous impulses go in the former, selfish impulses in the latter.

Parents who accept the theory of the divided self and the theory of the common good are nannies, and parenting for them means socializing children by teaching them how to enter into the tradition—adopt its values, succeed in its institutions, exhibit its virtues—by setting aside their own concerns when these conflict with what they have been taught is the common good. In this tradition teachers are nannies given the task of transmitting skills and the history and rationale of the tradition, and social workers, counselors, welfare workers, and police are nannies dealing with those who deviate from standard or approved procedures or simply cannot succeed within the accepted rules. Nannies tutor people in the art of being divided selves. These are well-meaning people, doing what they think best and often doing it well. But they are dangerous because they are perpetuating a false picture of human nature and a cramped view of the relationships we can establish with each other. They illustrate the fact that much that is done generously, sympathetically, out of concern for others, and with the best of good will, is hurtful.

## 2.9   Ethics as Networking

This classical view of desirable human relationships, deeply ingrained as it is in our culture, must constitute a problem for us. What Aristotle classed as a friendly act would be, for us, intrusive. We would not consider it friendly at all. Aristotle's friend, we would say, is a do-gooder imposing upon us his own idea of what is good for us. It is not *caring* that Aristotle was describing, but *caretaking*. That is a most important distinction for us. We treasure our independence, our way of life, and we resent it when others, no matter how well meaning, take it upon themselves to decide who we shall be or how we shall live our life. This is not simply a matter of "cussedness." We have adopted our way of life because it deals with what is most important to us. It embodies our priorities and helps us to deal with what we take to be the greatest threats to them. It gives us satisfactions we don't think we could find in any other way realistically open to us. It may not be perfect, but it is the best we have been able to work out.

Our reaction, then, is moral, a defense of our values. From this we must draw a surprising, if not shocking, conclusion. We are morally estranged from our classical tradition. We no longer share its moral ideals—perfectionism, absolute goods, hierarchically organized society, personality conceived as a struggle between reason and feelings. But this does not mean we are immoral. We have a different set of values. It is not so much that we have rejected traditional values as that they have gradually become irrelevant to our lives, our hopes, and our problems. The society in which they originated no longer exists. The transmutations have become overwhelming. We are different people, and the institutions which we have created and which we rely upon have new functions.

We are moderns, and we live in the modern world. That world is not subject to unchanging reason; it is a network of people managing their lives as well as they can. Our relationships are not those between wise masters and dutiful subordinates, but those of equals seeking understanding and support from one another. In a world still modernizing we are defending new values, values which sustain a richer and more ethical life, values which are better grounded. If we are not doing this—if we are, indeed, simply rebelling against strictures which seem to make no sense to us—it is because we have not created an ethics which incorporates the values that have emerged as so important in the modernizing world. Our moral confusion—and it is great—stems from the fact that our efforts to be ethical, since they are not in accord with the principles found in the classical worldview, are regarded as a rejection of ethics. This attitude, however, exactly reverses our real problem. What we need is an ethics which accepts our hopes and expectations as realistic. These are much higher than were those of people in earlier versions of our culture, and they are based in advances that have distanced us remarkably from earlier times. We have learned a great deal about nature and human nature; we have learned how to organize institutions to make them both more effective in accomplishing their aims and more responsive to our needs; we have broadened the participation of people in the development and management of social policies, and we have learned we can improve the quality of our lives. Central to these hopes and expectations is a new understanding of personality which rejects the classical model of human nature.

# 3.
# The Search for the Self

November 21, 1998

As the western world modernized, our understanding of what it means to be in and of the world did also. Up to this time nature had been viewed as a creation and living things as creatures; the creative force lay outside nature. Newton unsettled this worldview when he proclaimed "all the... motions in the world depend upon a certain kind of force." He meant a natural force, and he recognized that in adopting this position, he was assuming a responsibility to identify this force and show how it causes the motions we observe. The principle had philosophical as well as scientific implications: the power imputed to a creator was now to be replaced by one found in nature. Newton was well aware how radical his principle was; indeed, he was reluctant to accept it, both because he thought it would subject him to censure and because it conflicted with his own religious views. Although his notebooks reveal that he had adopted the principle before arriving at the "power laws" contained in his *Principia Mathematica*, published in 1687, he did not make it public until years later. He originally wrote the sentence quoted above for inclusion in an introduction to the first edition of his *Opticks*, which appeared in English in 1704, but he suppressed the introduction. Only in the second edition, published two years later in Latin, did he finally state it openly. Since then we have sought explanations by identifying forces in nature and describing how they work.

We saw in chapter 1 how difficult a task that is. Newton himself, burdened with metaphysical presuppositions carried over from classical times and theological beliefs grounded in them, did not succeed entirely, although he took the first and most difficult steps. In the long run, his greatest contribution was not his physics, important as that was, but the principle underlying it: *Natural events are energy in action.* While the universe is far more complex than Newton described it, it is, as he proclaimed, energy in action. If we now see it to be a dynamical system of dynamical systems, it is because we have pursued this insight of Newton's. It has taken three hundred years, and we have discovered that natural energies are interlocked, self-maintaining systems.

The same preconceptions which made it difficult for Newton to see the consequences of the principle for physical science were even more formidable when investigators turned their attention to the study of mind and personality. Human beings, after all, create and have value, and their spiritual life, it was almost universally believed, was beyond natural explanation. This view was contained in the well-entrenched Platonic belief that the soul is distinct from the body, of a different order, and unchanging. This near-universal belief, buttressed by ordinary language, which over the centuries had incorporated this view of things, made it nearly impossible to deny there is a self which has experience but is not that experience itself. From this viewpoint, mind was not a part of physical nature, and therefore personality was not a subject for scientific investigation. Thus a scientific, naturalistic account of personality, mind, and valuing came very late. Only in the 1880s and 1890s did William James and John Dewey succeed in constructing a naturalistic psychology. As they approached this task, they stood at much the same juncture with respect to personality as the one at which Newton had found himself as he studied physical nature two hundred years earlier. Like him, they sought explanations of experienced phenomena, and, like him, they believed those explanations would require identifying natural forces at work. Like him, they provided an excellent description, and, like him, they failed to identify the dynamic at work.

What made it possible for Dewey and James to create a naturalistic, scientific psychology was their rejection of the notion that there is a substantial self. They asserted that the self is psychical events themselves, interacting with each other and their surroundings, rather than a substance behind and underlying experience, serving somewhat as a pin cushion does pins which are stuck in it. As Dewey put it, "There is no ready-made self behind activities. There are complex, unstable, opposing attitudes, habits, impulses which gradually come to terms with one another, and assume a certain consistency of configuration." (Dewey [1922] 1930, 138) The self, he held, is that which it had been thought to have. As Gilbert Ryle put it in 1949, the notion that there is something behind experience manipulating it is "the dogma of a ghost in the machine." (Ryle 1949, 15–18) That dogma has now been put to rest, but it took decades. James and Dewey were philosophical psychologists, and so, while treating psychology as a science, they were alert to the philosophical implications of their theorizing. They knew that, in trying to explain personal experience without referring to a self behind it, they would seem to many to be denying that there is any spiritual, any truly worthwhile, life at all, for it was the substantial self which had been held to originate and sustain values. Without this "center," the self would appear to be merely an aggregate, a collection of psychical events without any real unity or permanence.

It was fortunate, in these circumstances, that William James should have been so sensitive to the importance and variety of the feelings and values that affect people most profoundly. He described the self as a "stream of thought," using a phrase which might at first blush be thought to make it sound dryly intellectual, but which, as he described it, did anything but. "A certain portion of the stream," he wrote, "is felt by all men as a sort of innermost centre within the circle, of sanctuary within the citadel, constituted by the subjective life as a whole." Speaking of this "innermost centre," he wrote, "Whatever qualities a man's feelings may possess, or whatever content his thought may include, there is a spiritual something in him which seems to *go out* to meet these qualities and contents, whilst they seem to *come in* to be received by it." (James 1890, 1:297) He was describing the self's peculiar quality of being both what is experienced and what is experiencing it. The stream of thought includes both the "qualities and contents" which "come in" and the "spiritual something" which "goes out" to meet them. As James pictured it, the self is vibrant, feelingful, and aspiring in a world which is full of obstacles and opportunities. There is, he wrote, a constant play of furtherances and hindrances in my thinking, of checks and releases, tendencies which run with desire, and tendencies which run the other way.... [These] reverberate backwards and produce what seem to be incessant reactions of my spontaneity upon them, welcoming or opposing, appropriating or disowning, striving with or against, saying yes or no. (1:299)

This spontaneity amid reverberating, pulsating feelings and thoughts creates a "palpitating inward life." (1:299) Life is the adventure of a spiritual being in a world which is both friendly and recalcitrant. The self James treated as a natural event was every bit as rich an object of investigation as it had been when viewed from other perspectives. Only its explanation was to change, and one test the explanation would have to meet was its ability to explain the self's rich variety.

## 3.1   WILLIAM JAMES, JOHN DEWEY, AND THE BEAR

The life of feelings posed this challenge directly. A century ago emotions were still being treated as bodily functions, as Plato had conceived them to be. They were physiological responses to physical events affecting the body, particularly those events warranting strong and immediate reactions, such as those commonly referred to as "fight or flight." James, regarding feelings as important components of the "inner core" of the self, could not accept emotions as merely bodily. They must be an essential part of personality itself. He therefore turned to the task of developing a theory of emotions.

James, of course, was strongly influenced by Darwin's theory of evolution. The nature he studied was anything but placid: organisms had to be constantly on the alert to deal with threats to their very existence. Those which did not cope with dangers died, and whole species could become extinct. To avoid this, plants and animals possessed responses which over geological time had proved adaptive. Many of these were instinctive in animals, and it was not unreasonable to expect that human beings, with their animal background, act instinctively also, at least in some circumstances. Noting that, given immediate and obvious dangers, neural and glandular reactions provide emergency energies for human beings as for animals, James listed a number of human instincts, each a patterned response programmed into the neurophysiological system so that it occurred automatically whenever triggered by an external object of a specific type, much as a piano produces a particular note when a key is struck. Human beings, he wrote, confronted with a danger, affront, or extreme disappointment, act "in such a way as to produce certain ends, without foresight of the ends, and without previous education in the performance." (2:383) A physical stimulus, he was contending, directly causes a physiological response. But the reaction is not simply physical: "every object that excites an instinct excites an emotion as well." (2:442) The physical and emotional responses are coterminous. In an emotional situation *"bodily changes follow directly the perception of the exciting fact, and... our feeling of the same changes as they occur is the emotion."* (2:449)

As James described them, the changes were in the body, the feelings in the mind. Mind and body were working in concert to produce behavior essential to the welfare of the individual. This, it readily can be seen, was entirely contrary to the traditional account. Whereas for Plato reason achieved the good by controlling and disciplining feelings, for James the self survived and prospered by using feelings as guides to action. The significance of James' revision of the traditional account was far-reaching. After this, the question was not whether reason could control emotions, but how feelings and thoughts could collaborate to constitute a self capable of dealing with difficulties ranging from the practical to the spiritual. James, bent on answering this question, stressed the connectedness of the several aspects of emotional experience. The physiological changes, such as hormonal discharges and the rush of blood, he wrote, "follow directly" the perception causing the emotion, and "every one of the bodily changes, whatsoever it be, is *felt*, acutely or obscurely, the moment it occurs." (2:450) In taking this position, James was reversing the common-sense account of the most basic emotions, and he knew it. "Common-sense says," he wrote, "we lose our fortune, are sorry, and weep; we meet a bear, are frightened and run; we are insulted by a rival, are angry and strike." Rather, "we feel sorry because we cry, angry because we strike, afraid because we tremble." (2:449–50) James' position was believable because of the directness of the response. The reaction to the bear, for example, seemed neither to require thought nor to allow time for it. Any criticism would have to take this immediacy and apparent spontaneity into account.

James' account related bodily changes to states of feeling so they each required and contributed to the other, but it did so in such a way as to raise doubts about the ability of an individual to direct his own affairs. It was the sequence as James described it which raised questions. As long as or to the extent his physical reactions were prior to or simultaneous with his feelings about them, one could not be said to be in control of his own actions. To use the frightful bear as an example: an individual's emotional response, to the extent it followed instinctively upon physiological changes, occurred without benefit of his evaluation of the danger or his judgment about how best to respond; it required no thought or prior experience. The reaction seemed not to be "his" at all. The spiritual quality of the feeling life James prized so highly appeared to be undermined by his theory of emotion.

John Dewey judged this account as unsatisfactory. "Hope, fear, delight, sorrow, terror, love, are too important and too relevant in our lives to be in the main the 'feel' of bodily attitudes which have themselves no meaning." (Dewey 1894, 563) An adequate theory of emotion would show why they are so meaningful a part of life. The key, Dewey suggested, lies in the fact that emotions, along with ideas and physiological changes, are parts of a coordinated, purposive activity. The attitude we have toward an event and the feeling we have about it are simultaneous, and they both reflect the aim directing our activity. The feeling is the "return wave" of the attitude, its "resonance." The "mode of behavior" is continuous and coordinated: in it an object comes to attention and creates tensions in the purposive activity. *"The idea and the emotional excitation are constituted at one and the same time; that indeed, they represent the tension of stimulus and response within the coordination which makes up the mode of behavior."* (Dewey 1895, 18–19) The tensions contain distinctions of value, and these are related to the aims directing the ongoing activity which has been interrupted and called in question. All of this occurs *within* the ongoing activity, but, within it, the physiological response carries into effect the valuations (feelings) and attitudes (ideas) creating this reverberating tension.

None of this can occur, however, except in the purposive activity which is ongoing and which, having been disrupted, must be reconstituted. The encounter with the bear didn't begin with the bear; it began with the organism making its way in its surroundings with purposes and understandings it had already achieved. The bear "breaks in" upon this ongoing experience, thus exciting the organism, which reacts in terms of its aims and memories. The bear is not a stimulus except as it interrupts the ongoing activities of the organism. The organism notes it *as an interruption*, thus turning it into a stimulus, in this case a threat. The stimulus, the threat, having broken into the ongoing activity, disturbing its behavior and perhaps calling its aims into question, poses a problem with which the organism must deal. The reflex-arc concept which James had used in his explanation Dewey characterized as "sensation-followed-by-idea-followed-by-movement." (Dewey 1896, 358). But, he argued, the emotional situation is not simply sequential. The process of moving from coordinated activity, to upset, to reconstituted coordinated activity, is circular, and he likened it to a circuit. "The arc... is virtually a circuit, a continual reconstitution" of ongoing activity. Such a circuit "is a co-ordination, some of whose members have come into conflict with each other." (Dewey 1896, 360, 370) Dewey was going beyond then-current analyses of experience in this explanation, and it is not entirely clear.

He seemed to think of the circuit as involving physical, physiological, and conscious energies. Their conjunction sets up "return waves" among them, and the ongoing activity is shaped by their reverberation. Feelings and attitudes are shaped in these vibrations and affect physical and physiological activities as well as feelings and attitudes.

The process is sequential, but it is a sequence of vibrations in which everything affects everything else and all the elements contributing to the situation are changed in their interadjustments. Dewey may not have recognized this full complexity at the time, and he certainly had no scientific evidence, or even scientific model, on which to make such inferences, but he was making a remarkably accurate account of networking reality. In experience the conscious act or effort is twofold: it gives the interrupting event a value and it cognizes it as an object. The agent characterizes the intrusion as an "object" and evaluates how it affects her welfare. In encountering the bear, for instance, she identifies the bear as a bear, that is to say, as something which does what a bear does, and, at the same time and as part of the same process, judges these bear-functions to be a danger to herself. The former aspect of this process is intellective, the latter affective. The bear is certainly a part of the exciting cause, but it doesn't become a stimulus except as a "frightful bear." As Dewey summed up his analysis, "The outcome of this co-ordination of activities constitutes, for the first time, the object with such and such an import—terrible, delightful, etc.—or [what is the same thing considered from a different perspective] constitutes an emotion referring to such and such an object.... The frightful object and the emotion of fear are two names for the same thing." (Dewey 1895, 20) The bear becomes frightful as the fright becomes a bear. Attitudes and feelings, in other words, both become what they are because of their relationship to the other.

The example was an especially good one because the emotion of fear was one of those emotions most often and easily regarded as purely physiological. If it was true here, it was true for any emotion that it involves a valuation and a judgment. In Dewey's analysis, an emotional reaction, while direct and often overpowering, requires judgment and evaluation. Furthermore, the judgment and valuation have to be collaborative: the evaluation depends upon the identification, the identification is colored by the evaluation. Feeling and thinking are generally collaborative in this way. The encounter with the bear is not different in kind from any other emotional experience, as both James and Dewey made clear by their choice of illustrations. James grouped the encounter with the bear with experiences such as being insulted or losing a fortune. An insult, though, does not pose a threat to our life, but to our self-esteem or reputation. Losing our fortune threatens our security, our living pattern, perhaps our standing in the community, but it poses no immediate threat to our life. Dewey's analysis would track these experiences just as well as the encounter with the bear. In fact, they perhaps make the point even better, for our reactions to these events tend to be more diverse, and this makes clear that they involve interpretation and evaluation. What is insulting to one person is not to another. What is insulting in one circumstance is not in another, even for the same person. We may even be insulted for another, e.g., for our child, even though the child does not detect the insult. What is considered a fortune by some is not for others. And whether the loss came as a result of our own miscalculations or through the machinations of others may make a profound difference in our reaction. The valuation and judgment, in other words, are linked and contextual. They are commentary upon our purposive activity and the basis for choosing its future course.

## 3.2   THE ELUSIVE SELF

Throughout their lives James and Dewey made explicit what they took to be the ethical and social implications of their psychological views. Conduct was what they studied as psychologists, but they always treated it as both the exercise ground for character and a revelation of it. Yet, in Dewey's case, there was a curious rift between the account he gave of human beings in his psychological writings and the account he gave in his ethical writings. In the *Ethics* he wrote with James H. Tufts in 1908 and totally recast in 1932, Dewey included a chapter dealing with "the moral self." Yet, almost never did he use the words "person" or "personality," and only rarely did he use the word "self," in his psychological writings. There he used language which seemed to ascribe agency, not to a person, but to almost anything else but—habit, impulse, intelligence, the organism, mind, psychical events, customs, and traditions were some of the terms he used. In his introduction to social psychology *Human Nature and Conduct*, written twenty years after his analysis of the encounter with the bear, there is no chapter devoted to the self or person and no mention of personality. There the coordinated activity he had analyzed in the 1890s became "conduct," which he described as "interaction between elements of human nature and the environment, natural and social." (Dewey [1922] 1930, 10) When Dewey republished the reflex-arc article of 1896 in 1931, he entitled it "The Unit of Behavior." Behavior or conduct was the topic he discussed in his psychological writings, rather than the self or personality. It was activity which was ongoing, conduct in which habit, impulse, and intelligence had a place, the organism which performed these functions, and society in which the organism achieved integration. Thus, although he dealt with "the ethical problems connected with the fact of selfhood" in his *Ethics* (Dewey and Tufts 1932, 336), he denied the "fact" in his psychological writings. For many readers of the latter, the question was, where in all this is a self, a mind, personality, a person?

The psychologist Gordon Allport concluded that Dewey did not have a theory of personality at all. Invited to evaluate Dewey's psychology in 1939, he pointed out that it was the organism rather than personality which Dewey claimed was integrated and that it was society which provided the materials for integration. Allport agreed fully that psychological processes cannot occur apart from either physiological or social processes, but he argued they are profoundly different from both and have a unity of their own. He quoted from Dewey's then most recent book (Dewey 1938, 57 n. 7) his statement, "I am not aware of any so-called merely 'mental' activity or result which cannot be described in the objective terms of an organic activity modified and directed by symbols—meaning, or language, in its broad sense." Allport considered this a denial that personality has a dynamic unity of its own; Dewey, he believed, had reduced it to organic processes on the one hand and social processes on the other. In Dewey's account the self vanished, Allport wrote, leaving only organisms and societies. What remained was a "biological-cultural human being." (Allport 1939, 279) There was no autonomous person left.

For anyone acquainted with Dewey's usual robust defense of his philosophy, his response to Allport's criticism comes as something of a shock. He simply admitted he had failed to develop an adequate theory of personality:

> In a desire to cut loose from the influence of older "spiritualistic" theories about the nature of the unity and stability of the personal self (regarded as a peculiar kind of substantial-stuff), I failed to show how natural conditions show support for integrated and potentially equilibrated personality patterns. (Dewey 1939, 555-56)

The admission needs to be read very carefully. Dewey did not deny there are "integrated and potentially equilibrated personality patterns." Indeed, he wrote extensively of them. What he acknowledged was his failure "to show how natural conditions show support for" them.

He was, in effect, acknowledging that he could not locate the dynamic which makes possible the personal activities he described. That dynamic is, of course, just what I have said we can now identify with the help of recent theories of nature and caring. Evaluating Dewey's psychology from a perspective made possible by these recent advances, I find the *description* Dewey offered of human conduct to be largely correct. In general, he succeeded in describing the psychical events which constitute the self and locating them in their functional relationships with each other, the organism, and the environment. But he did not identify psychical events coalescing as a self with unity and continuity of its own—and therefore distinguishable from the organism and society. As a result, his psychology remained incomplete, and distorted at certain key points. While he was clear in his ethics that there is a purposing agent directing affairs and responsible for his conduct, his psychology did not show how this could be. In a sense, he was ahead of his time: he was handicapped by the lack of a theory explaining how energies can autocatalyze to become self-maintaining at a more powerful energy level. He could not see, therefore, that the very processes he described were such as to create a self meeting its own needs and exerting its own force. Dewey, seeking a scientific psychology, was limited by the science of his time. The recent discovery that nature is a system of autopoietic systems opens up a new way to interpret the facts he described. We can now amend and strengthen his psychology by developing a new scientific interpretation of facts which remain largely as he described them. The result will be a stronger theoretical base for his ethics.

Dewey's exchange with Allport provides a good starting point for such a review and reinterpretation. It raised this question: Is there a self which has its own unity and which exerts a force identifiably different from those of the organism and the environment? We start, of course, with agreement that any such self must be a functional rather than a substantive unity, for James and Dewey, along with many other psychologists, were successful in accounting for personal activities without reference to a substantive self. Thus we are looking for a self consisting of unified directive processes not ascribable to "animal activities," social influences, or a combination of the two.

The question is not whether there are mental processes and events. Dewey clearly asserted their presence and stressed their importance. "Hearing, seeing, perceiving in general, reasoning...have distinctive qualities which... are to be termed mental and conscious." (Dewey 1931, 257, 269) The question is, rather, whether Dewey thought these mental qualities are those of an agent acting autonomously. Neither his account of the relation of psychical qualities to the organism nor his account of their relation to society supported this view. He was clear that mental processes are energies in action, but he took the energies to be organic. Mental processes in all their forms are "force, urgency." (Dewey [1922] 1930, 165) The structure "of the so-called mental process or conscious process... is furnished by the human organism, especially its nervous system." (Dewey 1931, 251) Organic energies which involve mental activities are behavioral rather than simply physiological, and behavior is "certain adjustmental types of animal activities." (Dewey and Bentley 1949, 148) Mental activities, thus, are bodily functions, but behavior involves changes in the environment as well as the organism, and so "the environment is just as much comprised within behavior as are organic processes." (Dewey 1931, 311) The environment is both physical and social, but the latter is much the more important with respect to mental activities, for meanings are discoverable only in social interactions (313). Society is a network of meanings, and

> every individual lives in the network as a part
> of it. The material of personal reflection and of
> choice comes to each of us from the customs,

traditions, institutions, policies, and plans of these large collective wholes. They are the influences which form his character, evoke and confirm his attitudes, and affect at every turn the quality of his happiness and his aspirations. (Dewey and Tufts 1932, 351)

Society is the source of ideas, standards, and obligations. The integration of desires and aims is effected by adopting and internalizing these social events.

Mental processes, then, are organic energies integrating meanings gained from and applied in society. Note that Dewey was saying more than that mental processes include organic functions and social activities; he was saying they are not functions of a mind. Our conscious activities do not constitute consciousness; our mental activities are not those of a mind. He took this position because he thought consciousness or mind would have to be detachable from its activities, i.e., substantive (Dewey and Bentley 1949, 108). He held in 1930 that conscious acts are "performed by every normal human being.... [But] what some psychologists have done is to shove a soul or consciousness under these acts as their author or locus." (Dewey 1931, 257) In 1948 he wrote in the same vein, "The living, behaving, knowing organism is present. To add a 'mind' to him is to try to double him up" (Dewey and Bentley 1949, 132) and thus continue a dangerous tradition. "The ancient custom... was to regard all behaviors as initiated within the organism, and at that not by the organism itself, but rather by an actor or resident of some sort—some 'mind,' or 'psyche,' or 'person' attached to it—or more recently at times by some 'neural center' imitative of the older residents in character." (130) He was led to the conclusion that intelligence is not ours originally or by production. "It thinks" is a truer psychological statement than "I think." Thoughts sprout and vegetate; ideas proliferate. They come from deep and unconscious sources.... The stuff of belief and proposition is not originated by us. It comes to us from others, by education, tradition and the suggestion of the environment. (Dewey [1922] 1930, 314)

Thoughts "sprout" and "proliferate," but they do not coalesce to become a mind, a self, an agent.

We can only conclude that Allport's criticism was justified. Dewey's "self" was "biological-cultural": the organism was modified directly as it came in contact with society. "As they enter into distinctive human associations strictly organic properties are modified and even transformed." (Dewey 1931, 85) Using language almost identical with that used by Allport in his criticism, Dewey wrote, "The structure of whatever is had by way of immediate qualitative [mental or conscious] presence is found in the recurrent modes of interaction taking place between what we term organism, on one side, and environment, on the other." (252–53) Even a decade after Allport made his criticism and Dewey accepted it, Dewey, with Bentley, held that "all... [man's] behavings, including his most advanced knowings, are activities not of himself alone, nor even primarily his, but processes of the full situation of organism-environment." (Dewey and Bentley 1949, 104; rephrased slightly) Desires, judgments and purposes may be "immediate qualitative experiences," but they are "physical and animal" and "awakened" by social influences.

This is only half the story, however, for Dewey's denial of the existence of a mind or self coexisted with a description of behavior which, considered apart from this denial, leads to an entirely different conclusion.

Throughout his life Dewey considered behavior as a self-maintaining, self-regulating system of energies. In an 1895 article, he used the analogy of a circuit to describe experience adapting itself to meet its needs in constantly changing surroundings. What he meant was that ongoing purposive activity is a "system of tensions" in equilibrium, channeled by habits but susceptible to events which exert force toward other objectives. The conflicting impulses and habits, themselves energies, interadjust to re-establish a new equilibrium. The ongoing activity undergoes shifts in tension but maintains an uneasy balance. He apparently felt increasingly that this view was correct, for when he reprinted the article in 1931 what he had called "virtually a circuit" in the original article he termed "actually a circuit." Such change in a system of tensions is just what we have learned to expect in any self-maintaining system as it balances centripetal and centrifugal forces. The conduct Dewey described was basically that of an autopoietic system. The interadjusting forces are conscious, events given a meaning and formed into habits, dispositions, or interests. Such a system usually responds to interference by returning to or close to its original trajectory; in this case most behavior is habitual. Sometimes, however, the disruption is of such a sort that a change of course is required to resolve the conflicting forces; in this case intelligence consists of precisely those habits or dispositions—resourcefulness, perseverance, inquisitiveness, generosity, sympathy, and their like—open to new aims and altered conduct. Dewey's description of mental activities is largely concerned with their integrative and self-corrective nature, the way they maintain balance through self-regulation and self-direction.

Habit operates when physiological, emotional, intellective, behavioral, and environmental elements have achieved a condition of equilibrium in which expectations, memories, and actions are adjusted to each other harmoniously. The equilibrium is of actions; habits bias conduct by creating "special sensitiveness." If we are inquisitive, we readily find things to question; if we are generous, we recognize many opportunities to be helpful; if we are moody, we encounter many depressing events. Such habits are more recognizable as dispositions. They are characteristic modes of response, traits of personality, qualities of character, or even virtues or vices. While Dewey considered them functions of the organism, we cannot explain how they have the effect they have unless we consider them functions of a self. It is a self which achieves balance, not a habit. It was not a habit or disposition which was upset at sight of a bear, but the individual who sighted it. It was an individual who had to make the proper inferences and take the appropriate action, for it was his safety which was threatened. Thoughts, feelings, and doings appear and operate in a circuit, as Dewey held, reinforcing and influencing each other, but their integration requires that they coalesce to become a self. The circuit is a self, a system of tensions balanced to maintain itself.

In all natural systems there is a "sensitivity" to certain things or events. The mouse is sensitive to the shadow which signals the presence of the hawk, the bee to the color of the flower containing the nectar for its honey. The sensitivity is to qualities or events which are supportive or threatening. So, too, for human beings, as

Dewey's account makes clear. Their needs and wants, and the aims and hopes they construct in dealing with them, sensitize human beings to events affecting their welfare. Impulses are aroused by disturbing events, and the sensory-motor system reacts. The event disturbing behavior arouses energies which must be used somehow by the very dispositions which, by giving the event meaning, have created the energy. The meanings are desires, impulses which, originally dispersive bursts of energy, now have an idea how they can be satisfied, an objective. Most often their force is joined with that of other desires to form interests. Interests integrate impulses into a set of attitudes and activities which are concerted and thereby strengthened to provide force and focus for the attainment of their objectives. But for Dewey such integrations of energies were simply interests, energies which incorporate socially defined meanings into organic functions; they were not further integrated to become a self. The process is entirely typical of autopoietic systems, but the analysis was incomplete.

The same incompleteness is observable in Dewey's account of intelligence. Desires are never completely integrated, and conflicts are inevitable. When conflicts among desires are so great that equilibrium is upset and ongoing activity halted or rendered unsatisfying, a problem arises. Subjectively, the individual cannot get what he wants or cannot decide what he wants, and so is restive, confused, at odds with himself. Objectively, he cannot settle upon a course of action which is satisfying and effective. The conflict of desires can be resolved only by deliberation. Deliberation occurs when dispositions review the situation, balance the desires pressing upon them, consider the options available, and choose the course of action thought to be best suited to satisfy needs and maximize satisfactions. Its function is to renormalize, equilibrate, the flow of desires. "Reasonableness is in fact a quality of an effective relationship among desires rather than a thing opposed to desire." (Dewey [1922] 1930, 194) In dynamical terms, this is the appropriate interpretation. A resolution of conflicts is just that; anything else is control from outside. Yet Dewey did not recognize that reasonableness is a quality or state of a self resolving a difficulty it was experiencing and dealing with. He refused to refer to conscious activities as processes, because this might imply they are not functions of the organism.

Everything Dewey wrote about how intelligence resolves problematic situations, however, was consistent with a dynamical explanation. The dispositions at work, ideally, are "plastic to the transforming touch of impulse," (102) or desire, and their task is to "renew disposition and reorganize habits." (170) In other words, energies are to be used to renew energies, dispositions to revise themselves to make them effective in altered circumstances. "Scientific inquiry, artistic production, social companionship possess this trait to a marked degree." (143) They are "creative" activities because they bring along with them "a release of further activities." Such a creative move is growth. "We set up this or that end to be reached, but the end is growth itself." (Dewey and Tufts 1932, 340) Growth is the ideal, and growth is the use, and thereby the development, of the dispositions which further growth, those constituting intelligence. The circuiting of energies in this process of adjustment is evident. Intelligent behavior is both the outcome sought and the means of achieving it. The spiraling characteristic of natural systems is obvious in this account of personal development.

Dewey ran into difficulties, however, when he tried to show how people for whom growth was the good harmonized desires in a satisfying life—that is, how growth could serve as the basis for improving personal and social life. That he thought it must do so is clear. We judge our desires and interests, he wrote, by

> detecting the different courses to which they commit us, the different dispositions they form and foster, the different situations into which they plunge us.
>
> In short, the thing actually at stake in any serious deliberation is... what kind of person one is to become, what sort of self is in the making, what kind of a world is making. (Dewey [1922] 1930, 216–17)

The biological model Dewey was using proved insufficient for this purpose. Growth, as Dewey used the term, served to describe a process of interaction between organism and environment analogous to that found in then-current biological theories. According to that theory, organisms survive in a competitive struggle for scarce resources. The environment makes demands upon organisms, which the organisms must satisfy. The environment changes, shifting its requirements and weeding out as "unfit" those which are unable to meet the revised requirements. Organisms are part of the environment for other organisms, and the struggle for survival is sometimes among organisms and species. Each type of organism has characteristic functions by which it remains viable. Organismic functions use environmental resources and encounter environmental obstacles. It is the environment which selects the organism for survival or selects it for extinction. We can see here the influence of Newton's classical model, in which bodies were moved by external forces and had no force or direction of their own.

For an organism, continued successful adaptation in varying conditions is viability, not growth. An organism remains viable by making successful adaptations. Dewey knew very well that personal development, what he called growth, is more than adaptation to external forces, but his theoretical model betrayed him. It left no room for the reform of society which was so prominent a concern of his. The fault lay in his conception of the self as organic-social, that is, his view that the human organism is changed directly by social influences. But this provides no standard by which to judge people if they are considered responsible. To say that growth, conceived as the internalizing of standards existing in society, is the end is to remove any basis for judging "what kind of person one is to become." For other organisms viability is the sign of success, but human beings establish aims *within* life. Further life is not the end; ethics, and intelligence also, have a place only within life.

The biological model Dewey used undercut his social theory just as it did his theory of personality. Just as Dewey set out to show that ethical behavior is found in persons who are directing their affairs intelligently to become free and responsible but failed to show how this could be, so also he set out to show that only a democratic and scientific society fosters intelligence but ended up claiming that agreement is required of all. In his psychology the failure followed from his inability to conceive a self with needs and abilities distinct from and distinctively different from those of the organism. In his social philosophy the failure followed from his inability to distinguish this same self from the social influences playing upon it.

His start was promising. He began by noting a tension existing in modern life. On the one hand, individuals are social beings: "men have to act together, ... and their conjoint action is embodied in institutions and laws" (Dewey and Tufts 1932, 351), which impose obligations and grant rights that govern relationships. On the other hand, there is disagreement about what these obligations and rights are, at least in modern western society, and individuals must decide "what social tendencies they shall favor and... which institutions they shall strive to conserve." (352) He was a pluralist trying to break away from · the tradition in which personal obligations are derived from a conception of a common good in the face of which personal desires are to be set aside.

Freedom and responsibility are the traits sought in citizens, and the ideal society will support their "possibility of growth, learning and modification of character" (339) by being scientific and democratic. Dewey was using both words in an unusual way. To be scientific was to be experimental, open-minded: people should "exhibit willingness to reexamine and if necessary to revise current convictions, even if that course entails the effort to change by concerted effort existing institutions." (366) To be democratic was to exhibit "a positive toleration which amounts to sympathetic regard for the intelligence and personality of others." (365) In this ideal community "each contributes something distinctive from his own store of knowledge, ability, taste, while receiving at the same time elements of value contributed by others." (383)

The balance here appears to be perfect between, on the one hand, personal freedom and responsibility and, on the other, full participation in a community of persons of varying abilities and differing opinions.

When, however, Dewey went on to describe how such a society could be achieved, he drew a somewhat different picture. The satisfaction of individuals is not the standard against which events and institutions are to be judged. "Regard for self and regard for others are both of them secondary phases of a more normal and complete interest: regard for the welfare and integrity of the social groups of which we form a part." (337) In taking this position, Dewey made clear the implications of saying that the self is "integrated" by accepting the ideas, standards, and obligations imposed upon it by society. It is the welfare and integrity of the group which is primary, not that of its members. The "problem of morals is to form an original body of impulsive tendencies into a voluntary self in which desires and affections center in the values which are common." (336) Calling the action voluntary only disguised the move. Dewey was invoking the common good, the standard which has always been used, sooner or later, to impose uniformity of conduct and unanimity of belief, with disastrous effects. Accepting it, he extolled "a type of individual whose pattern of thought and desire is enduringly marked by consensus." (Dewey 1962, 89) In the end, Dewey's social theory contained irreconcilable elements. Its primary thrust was toward a pluralistic society in which personal responsibility consisted of voluntary participation in the institutions of an open society. The ideal was beautifully framed. Even the "common good" was defined in a pluralistic fashion. It would not be good if it was achieved "at the expense of the active growth of those to be helped" or common if they "have no share in bringing about the result." (Dewey and Tufts 1932, 385) Yet, finally, Dewey could find no way of realizing this society except by achieving consensus. Starting out with the fact of disagreements, he could not find a positive place for them; they must be either tolerated or eliminated.

It might be argued that the agreement would be only to create an open and democratic society, but this does not remove the problem. To claim as ideal a society which opens the way for its members to achieve their own good merely shifts the problem to the individual members, who must then determine what their good is to be; but we have seen that the personal good is only continued growth. To claim, on the other hand, that the personal good is growth which is to be achieved by accepting socially defined standards, merely shifts the problem to society, which must then determine what the common good is to be; but we have seen that full participation and further experimentation is all that is proposed. The two theories fit together but provide no answer. To recommend viability and consensus with others tells us only that Dewey meant it when he asserted that conscious processes "take place between what are the organism, on one side, and environment, on the other." There was no self, only these two in interaction.

It must be clear that Dewey was never entirely successful in solving the problem which confronted him from the beginning, namely, describing a self which is processual rather than substantive. The difficulty lay, it seems apparent now, in the lack of any conception of how energies such as those he located could achieve a functional unity through purely natural processes. We can readily sympathize with him. He wanted a naturalistic explanation and thought it must be scientific, but science had not yet provided the basis for one. He was ahead of his time. Although he knew nothing of autopoietic natural systems, his description traced the outlines of such a system. Throughout his account of the interadjusting activity of what he called "the elements of human nature," Dewey described them as energies, sometimes conflicting, sometimes coalescing, always seeking equilibrium, integration. The energies existed in a "system of tensions" and sought a resolution of forces which would leave them more energetic and more unified as dispositions created sensitivities which triggered stimuli which activated dispositions to equilibrate the competing impulses in reorganized dispositions. Energies expended themselves to create new, redirected energies. Energies were increased and redirected as obstacles created tensions so great a choice had to be made.

Dewey did not know that such circuiting occurs when energies autocatalyze, creating a system of delicately balanced forces, a new unity with its own requirements for self-maintenance and a new system of forces released into its surroundings in order to meet its needs, nor did Allport. It is worth noting that Allport, in the same article in which he criticized Dewey for failing to identify a continuous and unitary self, found fault with his theory of behavior as circuiting energies. His objection was the same as that made by physicists and biologists to evidence of similar networking in physical and biological events: if this is what is going on, analysis is impossible. "Evolving circuits," Allport wrote, "may indeed be, as Dewey insists, the course of mental life, but spiraling processes make orderly analysis in terms of separate variables impossible." He was aghast at Dewey's picture of "the reciprocal interpenetration of impulse, habit and thought, the continuous relating of these functions with the properties of the environment, which in turn is regarded as continuously evolving in terms of the properties of both the organism and the environment as related." He exclaimed in consternation, "such a flux of processes and events"! (Allport 1939, 288) The reaction was ironical, for, while criticizing Dewey for failing to assert the existence of persons as self-directing agents, he was also calling him to task for describing precisely the networking energies of personality essential to an autonomous, self-directing person.

In assessing Dewey's contribution to philosophy we have a vantage point we gain from the introduction of a dynamical systems theory of nature and a companionate theory of caring. These are both developments that have occurred since his time, and they allow us to achieve what he set out to do but failed to do. In fact, we find ourselves in a somewhat paradoxical position. There has been a "return to Dewey" in philosophical circles in recent years, but little explanation of why his thought again appears persuasive. In light of these recent developments, however, this becomes clear. Recent scientific thought has advanced a point of view he advocated, namely, the interdependence and interadjustment of entities of all kinds, but now with an explanation. *All* entities are now recognized as processes which achieve their characteristic mode of operation in a dynamical balance with other entities in a networking of energies. Each becomes itself as it contributes to the dynamical balance of the other participants in the network.

The integrity of each is achieved in the like achievement of the integrity of the others. We have described Dewey's philosophy as containing a split caused by his failure to conceive the self as a processual, dynamically balanced unity of this sort. Though he described mental or conscious processes as having a unity, he assigned the energies used to the organism and the unity achieved to society. He ended with consensus as a condition for the flowering of individuality, an incoherent solution of an all-important problem.

With the perspective provided by the dynamical systems theory of nature and the theory of companionate caring, we can now describe the self as experience rather than as a substance underlying or behind experience. It is, as Dewey stated, "complex, unstable, opposing attitudes, habits, impulses which gradually come to terms with one another, and assume a certain consistency of configuration." (Dewey [1922] 1930, 138) But it is no longer simply the behavior of an organism achieving its unity by entering into a social consensus. It is now a self, a natural entity in a natural network. If personality is organized and functions as other natural events do, we have the basis for a more coherent account of personality than Dewey provided and a stronger basis for the ethical and social ideals Dewey supported.


## 3.3   FROM BEHAVIOR TO SELF

All natural systems have a characteristic way of maintaining themselves. We should expect, therefore, that human beings function in a typical and distinctive fashion. We sometimes describe the characteristic way a system functions by identifying what it "seeks"; an organism, we say, "seeks" to remain viable. Such a phrasing is figurative when used of other types of autopoietic systems, it merely records what happens, but human beings do in fact seek ends they are conscious of. What is it that human beings seek?

In answering this question, we can accept in modified form Dewey's reiterated claims that behavior uses organic energies and the environment lies "within" behavior. Any natural entity exists in a form which reorganizes the energies it autocatalyzes and depends upon the transfer of energies to and from other entities with which it is coupled in such a way that they are both "inside" and "outside" it. Thus we should expect to find that the self uses organic energies reorganized and that it carries out its functions by coupling with other natural systems, including human beings.

The self incorporated many physical and physiological features as it autocatalyzed in the distant past. The size of the brain cavity, the structure of the larynx, the capacity for stereoscopic vision, and the slant of the pelvis are only a few of the features that have been held to be essential to selfhood of the human kind; in all likelihood all of them and others were required. Whatever the route and the crucial elements, the self appeared and is developed anew in each infant. The requisite capacities for feeling and thought are present at birth, although not a self. That appears out of the feelings and thoughts as these are complicated and integrated in a natural, indeed, inevitable, learning process. A newborn infant can satisfy its initial, organic needs only by assigning them meanings in a process which creates new needs and new satisfactions. When it experiences contractions of its stomach muscles, it *feels* uncomfortable. It becomes restless, is fed, repeats the process, and soon *learns* to focus its efforts upon certain features of its environment which seem related to relief of its discomfort. The discomfort has been given a meaning, hunger, with which it can deal. It cannot respond to the spasms of the stomach muscles, it can only respond to the hunger it feels, i.e., the meaning it learns to give the experience (Dewey 1925, 317–18). But in the process, it has increased, complicated, and organized its needs and converted them into desires. Soon enough the infant recognizes the desires as its own, that is to say, becomes *self*-conscious. Selfhood depends upon consciousness of this self-referential type. All autopoietic systems are self-referential, but the self-reference of a human being is unique because it is conscious. Most natural systems are not conscious at all; some are conscious, and a few *may* be self-conscious. But no others are self-conscious in the way human beings are. We watch the peacock strut, but we doubt that he knows or cares whether he is beautiful. We watch chimpanzees groom each other, but we don't know whether they have chosen to do this, and we are pretty sure they don't do it in order to be pretty or healthy, although that may be the result. The self-reference of a natural system does not require consciousness; when we said earlier that the immune system "recognizes" itself, we were using metaphorical language. The circulatory system doesn't know it is a circulating system, and a chimpanzee doesn't make a decision to be this or that kind of chimpanzee. Among natural systems a human being is distinctive because it is conscious of what it does and feels and is able to change its ways.

These abilities are made possible by the dual reference of the self-consciousness of a human being. The self is aware of objects, and it is aware of itself being aware of them. We not only know, we know that we know and what we know; we not only act, we know that we act and how we act; we not only feel, we know that we feel and how we feel. Dewey did not fully appreciate this. As he sought to show that the environment lies within behavior, he pointed out that "attitudes, dispositions and their kin.... are always *of, from, toward* situations and things." (238) In other words, we are always attending to something "out there," beyond us. While this is true, it is equally the case that attitudes, dispositions, etc., are *for, of,* and *by* a self dealing with the situations and things. This latter aspect of consciousness is just as immediate, direct, and important as the former. When we are hungry, we are as important an aspect of the experience as the food. When we receive a compliment, the fact that it is directed at us is essential to the experience. When we perform a service, it is ours and this determines its quality for us as much as does the benefit for its recipient. Every experience engages the agent and its surroundings in a reciprocal relationship; what happens to its surroundings alters the situation for the self, and what happens to the self alters its circumstances. Our consciousness places us as active participants in this exchange.

At the organic level, this is obvious. The beating of the heart depends upon taking oxygen from the surroundings and discharging carbon dioxide into them. The sudden appearance of a bear leads to a quickening of the heartbeat and a man-bear duet of mutually conditioning actions. Meanings govern and interpret such balletic sequences, and the pace quickens as each event sets off a cascade of further events. William James, describing consciousness of a relatively simple sort, referred to the way in which the contents of the stream of thought "reverberate backwards to produce what seem to be incessant reactions of my spontaneity." (James 1890, 1:299) Dewey, considering the same events, referred to their "resonance," to the presence of "return waves" in what appeared to be a "circuit" which constantly altered the "system of tensions." The changes "spiraled," because the tension was never twice quite the same; changes accumulated, to become trends.

Their descriptions fit the activity observable in a network. Every network is operationally closed. Its reverberations turn energies back upon their source to power its further functioning, thus giving the networking its unity and continuity. Self-consciousness is such a networking system. Its resonating thoughts and feelings are the meanings which are united and continued. The self, mind, or consciousness is these meanings in their processual integrity. Networks are also joined with other networks, other systems; they are organizationally open. This permits each system to be effective beyond its own "boundaries," but the effectiveness is a function of its own self-sustaining force. In a network, participating units and their relationships are both strengthened. Consciousness can be shared, but it cannot be merged with other minds. The sharing of thoughts and feelings and the autonomy of the minds in which they exist are correlates; each depends upon and furthers the other.

As a natural system, a self is a tightly coiled bundle of energies. It is a system of energies in tension, networking to maintain their delicate balance. There are a number of tensions contained in self-consciousness.

The first of these we have noted already. The self encounters its surroundings as an other, and each gains meaning in their interadjustment. The other, being what it is and responding as it does, conditions the self, which uses and incorporates it. The tension is unavoidable: there could be no self without the other, nor any other without the self. Although much more complicated, the situation is like what occurs when a note is struck. Waves appear, and overtones are created as these waves rebound and intermingle. The note and its surroundings combine to this effect. So in consciousness! The self and other are united in a balance so delicate that almost anything can change them.

A second dimension is added to this balance by the fact that consciousness is both intellective and emotive. The self, in recognizing an object, is conscious of what it is and does and also aware that it, the self, is aware of it. The self, in responding emotionally, assesses the object's impact upon the self's welfare. We have already noted that Dewey recognized this duality within conscious activity. You will recall that, in unraveling what takes place in an unexpected encounter with a bear, he maintained the intellective aspect of the act is a matter of gaining information, the affective aspect a matter of evaluating that information. Specifically, the former identifies the bear as a bear, the latter judges it a danger. The latter, he wrote, is a *"valuation... in terms of our own inner welfare."* (Dewey 1895, 21–2; italics added) Both emotion and intellect refer to both the self and surrounding events. There are two sets of tensions, and they are in tension with each other. It is as if two notes have been struck. The overtones multiply; harmonies and dissonances appear. There are, you might say, two axes, two dimensions, and a network is created. What is important to us influences what we pay attention to, which influences what we come upon, which influences how we think we are progressing, and so on: The cycling is never-ending. Each judgment contains a valuation, each valuation a judgment. "Circular logic" prevails. The self spirals as it seeks an integration of feelings and thoughts which relates it productively to its surroundings and furthers its welfare. Even for an infant, the reverberations are transforming. His discomfort is the occasion for feeding, communicating, entering into a social relationship, becoming dependent upon the food source, gaining some control over his surroundings, associating satisfactions with their context, developing competence and confidence, trusting another, giving and gaining affection, bonding with another, appreciating food and affection, and gaining a sense of worth. Even in satisfying purely organic needs, the infant creates new sensitivities, new connections, new forms of satisfaction, new competencies, and new forms of response, all of which feed back to all the others in return waves which contribute to the formation of characteristic patterns of activity and the qualities of an emerging self. The process is life-long and becomes more complicated and more constructive with experience.

The self does not appear in the network; it *is* the networking. Dewey was correct. The self can be nothing other than its functions. There is no self behind experience, detached from it. The self is the experiencing, and experience is the reverberating intellective-affective activity resonating with the interadjusting self and world. But the fact that this experiencing is self-referential, self-maintaining, self-directing networking makes for a much more complicated situation than Dewey pictured. Reluctant to admit the presence of a self, Dewey claimed thought "directs" activity. Of the "elements of human nature," habit, impulse, and intelligence, habit and impulse, he wrote, are thoughtless; only thoughts can think. But thoughts don't think, either. Thoughts, impulses, and dispositions coalesce in consciousness to create a new unity. Only in the conscious activity of a self are impulses given meaning, for the meaning has to do with the welfare of the self. Only then do habits form, for they are the continuity of the self's meaningful experience. Only then do thoughts appear, for they deal with problems that arise only in assessments of a self interadjusting with the world. It is only the self which thinks. The problems which Dewey said trigger thoughts are problems only for a self with aims and feelings; the feelings aroused by the disturbances which create the problems are those of the self; the thoughts which respond to and "solve" the problems are the thoughts of the disturbed self. Dewey was right in holding these are inseparable parts of one act, but he was wrong in thinking they were functions of an organism. The act is that of a self.

The self is the reverberations of feelings with thoughts, consciousness of self with consciousness of other, and feelings/thoughts with self-other judgments and valuations. It is clearly distinguishable from, though not separable from, the organism and its surroundings. Its unity and continuity are its networking, a coiled tension of meanings with unmistakable force and direction. The strength of emotional responses, particularly those occasioned by events impacting upon its own welfare, and the originality displayed by its intelligence, are too strong, too obviously self-directing, to exist in a fusion of "biological-cultural" forces. Still, these features are not dissimilar in kind from those found in some other organisms. We see in the behavior of pets reactions of the same kind, although with a highly constricted range. And we test the "intelligence" of rats and apes. There are further complexities found in the self-consciousness of human beings providing the abilities, qualities, and conduct which are specifically human.

Whereas other organisms make adjustments which allow them to survive and meet needs and wants over which they have little control, human beings seek, not survival, but their own welfare. They try to improve the *quality* of their lives, to make them more meaningful. The difference between human beings and other living beings is as remarkable as that between living and nonliving things. We can acknowledge the difference by calling human beings *persons*. Persons can seek a life of improved quality because their networking self-consciousness is more complex than that of other organisms. It contains additional sources of tension, which open persons to a new dimension of experience, qualitative in its nature, with its own opportunities and dangers.

## 3.4   FROM SELF TO PERSON

A life of higher quality is one of greater satisfaction. Some other organisms seek satisfactions, but the satisfactions they seek and the methods they use to gain them are both limited, dictated by instincts. Neither feeling nor intelligence is so limited for human beings. Their emotional assessments are not simply about isolated events, but about a much more complex "inner welfare." Through intelligence they can imagine worlds different from the one they come upon and make changes so the latter conforms more closely to the former. This gives them much more flexibility. They invent and discover new satisfactions, and they create new ways of gaining satisfactions. Satisfactions, once achieved, serve as benchmarks for what experience can be like; lacking or lost, they require effort and ingenuity to be regained. In seeking satisfaction, people soon find some solutions are incorrect, that is to say, unsatisfying. From then on, their judgments are based on their conception of what is *satisfying* and what is *effective* in gaining satisfactions. The crucial experiences are those of *being satisfied* and *being wrong*. The first grows out of the kind of experience a newborn infant has as he, with the help of others, overcomes feelings of discomfort and distress. The second comes later, as the infant learns that some things work and some don't. The two experiences, rebounding upon each other, provide a basis for judging the quality of our lives; it sets our aims up as tests against which we can judge our success in reaching them and our conduct as a test of the feasibility of our aims.

Judgments of satisfaction and effectiveness reverberate, with each affecting the other. Our satisfactions are instrumental in guiding us in choosing courses of conduct; our conduct is instrumental in achieving satisfactions. In seeking more effective courses of conduct, we may discover new and deeper satisfactions. In seeking satisfactions, we may discover new and better courses of conduct. What we are interested in influences what is satisfying, which causes us to learn new techniques, which affects our conception of ourselves, which creates new interests, through which we find new satisfactions: The networking goes on and on, now more complicated with this dimension added. We spiral upwards as our understanding becomes more comprehensive and better grounded and our conduct becomes more satisfying and productive. These resonating thoughts and feelings reverberate with those on the intellective-affective and the self-other axes. They are not simply added to the other; they enter into them, improving the quality of judgments and assessments and thus enriching experience.

The spiraling is furthered by errors and disagreements. From the beginning, when newborn infants and their caretakers are together trying to identify sources of dissatisfaction and ways of overcoming them, they disagree and make mistakes. Both the disagreements and errors are about what is satisfying and how satisfactions can be gained. Because satisfactions and dissatisfactions are central to the quality of life and achieving the one and lessening the other are so important, the disagreements are intense and the mistakes disheartening. Emotions are aroused and another tension comes into play, that between one person and others. The earliest satisfactions an infant knows are those he discovers with the help of others, and usually they are satisfactions found in his relations with another. The earliest disagreements have been with these same others. Disagreeing about both what is satisfying and how satisfactions can be gained, people find their desires and practices conflict with those of their associates. No participant in a network achieves perfection as it adjusts to accommodate both its own needs and those of the other participants. And so the self-other tension becomes a highly personal matter, a person-person tension. While many disagreements can be resolved, the fact of disagreement will always be present. The creativity of the person-person tension is directed at living with disagreements as well as removing them.

In the face of disagreements of such importance,

communication is a vital necessity. What we can call the human conversation is an elaboration of discussions on these topics. It is not just about how to avoid leopards and find beehives—threats to life or limb and hints about survival techniques. It is about the quality of life for a creature delicately attuned emotionally and able to take advantage of complicated causal and imaginary relationships, and so communication has to be precise and detailed. Conversation in which people discuss their views about what is satisfying and how satisfactions can be gained creates return waves affecting judgments and valuations made in dealing with all the other tensions. The spiraling in which we shape ourselves and our surroundings becomes even more complex. We mentioned earlier that even in trying to satisfy the most basic physical needs, infants learn many things, for example, that they are dependent upon others, that they can get and give affection, and that they can manage some things. The learning occurs most rapidly when the discussion deals with disagreements and errors. We learn through our mistakes and, fortunately, through the mistakes of others. Since there is always more to learn and there are always greater satisfactions to be gained, the spiraling continues throughout life.

Since every satisfaction affects and is affected by our many other desires, as well as by many circumstances in our surroundings, we have to fit each one into our way of doing things or change one or the other. How we resolve such conflicts affects all our aims, hopes, principles, anxieties, doubts, responsibilities, attitudes, and theories, which, of course, are fitted together as patterns of conduct, traits of personality, and qualities of character. Gaining satisfactions, it turns out, is no simple matter.

Some of them are more important or more desirable than others; some come with unpleasant consequences. That is, some are more worthwhile than others. Once we find they have side effects and vary in quality, we realize we have to make choices among them. And so still another set of tensions is set up. Judgments of satisfaction are in a dynamical balance with judgments of worthwhileness. In the extreme, we find ourselves concluding that some satisfactions are not worthwhile, and we reject them. Worthwhileness becomes a new standard, one by which we select from among satisfactions, but it does not replace satisfyingness. Rather worthwhileness and satisfyingness create a new tension in our lives as each makes its judgment of the other. Perhaps in a perfect world, one in which we could all have everything we wanted, what is satisfying would be worthwhile and what is worthwhile would be satisfying, but in our workaday, imperfect world, they exist in creative tension. What is satisfying gains that status partly because it is worthwhile, while what is worthwhile gains that status partly because it is satisfying, but nothing is ever perfectly satisfying or perfectly worthwhile. Our effort to improve the quality of our lives requires greater integration of these two, sometimes incompatible, qualities.

Of all the standards we apply in making this effort, none has been subject to more persistent efforts to extract it from networking reality than has worthwhileness. Moralists have attempted to find a value which provides an absolute standard, one which trumps all other considerations. But there is no such value or set of values. All of the interadjustments in a network are imperfect and temporary, and this holds true for networking consciousness. This is not a defect; the unpredictable effect of "return waves" in a network follows from the fact that they are sometimes nonlinear; in human experience this is creativity. For persons everything is subject to change in a continuity which is always changing and a unity which is always partial. In managing our personal lives, we cannot take into account all the relevant factors, present and future, and so worthwhileness and satisfyingness are in a tension from which we cannot escape. This further complicates our lives. Every judgment becomes one which weighs many values, and every feeling assesses our achieved character against a standard we have set for ourselves but have not reached. We must decide, not only what others want and do so in light of the lives they want and the persons they want to be, but also against the life we want and the person we want to be.

Such satisfaction-worthwhileness and person-person judgments, when combined with all the others, bring the person to the fore as a directive force. Our networking is the way we manage our lives, and we gradually discover we are not just coming to terms with our surroundings— we are also deciding who we are going to be and how we can make our situation more satisfying and worthwhile. We find that we can't gain the satisfactions we want or do what we think will be worthwhile unless we have particular competencies and personal qualities, and so, whatever we do, we confront the problem of deciding what kind of person we are going to be. The problem won't go away. We are caught in a circle, or rather a spiral. We must discover what we must be like as we seek our satisfactions, and we can only find out what is satisfying as we use the qualities we have. When we are dissatisfied, we alter our way of doing things, drop some personal qualities for others, or change our mind about what is satisfying. The round is endless.

We are finding another source of tension—between decisions about satisfaction-worthwhileness and decisions about what our personality and character should be. In seeking a better life, we adopt patterns of conduct, traits of personality, and qualities of character we find satisfying and worthwhile. Nothing could be more important or require greater sensitivity. We pattern our responses, and if they are successful, we become more sensitive, more perceptive, more discriminating, and lay ourselves open to more problems, more pleasures and pains, and more ways of doing things. The more our feeling life grows, the more we have to think about; the more successful we are in solving our problems, the wider becomes the range of our interests. We appreciate more as we learn how to use things; we find more uses for them as we appreciate things. The more we find our successes represent the achievements of the person we think we are and want to be, the more confident and competent we become. These are personal characteristics, and we are persons. We don't choose to be persons; being a self of the human kind requires us to become a person. We cannot satisfy the most basic—and morally most innocent—need without entering into a process involving choices between better and worse and thus becoming a certain kind of person.

A person is a networking of energies seeking a release which will balance the many tensed values in a resolution which takes each into account in an appropriate way. A person seeks satisfaction and finds this sets him upon a dialectical path. This is a spiraling in which he uses every discovery as, not only a resolution of conflicting perceptions, feelings, valuations, beliefs, etc., but also as a launching pad for further discoveries. What has been discovered changes all of one's understanding and thus establishes a new ground for feeling and thought. The creativity revealed in the process is hard to imagine and, understandably, has been consistently underestimated. We can be more specific, though. Whether we start with a single desire or disappointment, we find the spiraling involves us in deciding what our life should be like and that this depends upon who we become. Seeking satisfactions of the simplest sort sets us on a course which requires us to take charge, take responsibility for what we do and what, within our power, happens.

We have described a very complex process, but we have not offered a prescription for either the kind of person we should be or the kind of life we should lead. In stressing the endless spiraling we sound very much like John Dewey declaring that growth itself is the end we should seek. Is spiraling for the sake of spiraling? I think not. As natural systems persons are seeking a life of higher quality. There is a normative standard implicit in the very idea of personhood. Since being a person is a process, the process must exhibit the qualities to be achieved. Since the process is networking, it must strengthen both the unity of the network and its relationship to the coupled networks. The network is the self, and to strengthen its unity is to strengthen the values, attitudes, and feelings we have discovered in self-consciousness, while to strengthen its relationships is to strengthen its bonds with other persons, other selves, and the natural world.

This is, of course, what the western tradition, following Plato, has said cannot be done, but we have the benefit of Nel Noddings' redescription of caring. That discovered in the nurturing found in companionate caring a dynamic which did exactly this. It allowed both the one caring and the one cherished to become more themselves while creating a strong and mutually sustaining bond between them. If her analysis is correct and I am right that a new ethics and social philosophy are implicit in it, we have the basis for believing that free and responsible persons can form democratic societies of people who differ and disagree. Members of such a society will have to determine in what their responsibilities consist and what kinds of practices and institutions are compatible with and sustain them, but they will know that both personal and social decisions must be nurturing. This cannot be considered a realistic hope, however, unless caring becomes generalized to such an extent that it affects personality and character.

While Noddings described a personal relationship, there is a general attitude which originates in and fosters caring. That is *concern*. We can get an idea how cultivating concern solves problems Dewey could not solve, and thus strengthen his philosophy, if we consider his alternative.

When Dewey described the way individuals focus their energies, he wrote of desires gathered into dispositions and dispositions, in turn, gathered into interests. Interest, for Dewey, was the attitude or motive which directs one's attention to an object, objective, or subject-matter. Children would learn if they took an interest in a topic or problem; thus the teacher's task was to kindle interest. But this was only an example; anyone acts to satisfy his interest. To illustrate what he meant by interest, Dewey quoted approvingly John Stuart Mill's (1864,

20) statement, "The cultivated mind... finds sources of inexhaustible interest in all that surrounds it; in the objects of nature, the achievements of art, the imaginations of poetry, the incidents of history, the ways of mankind past and present, and their prospects in the future." One pursues interests actively, even aggressively. It is strong motivation, but, while adequate for formal education and many other purposes, it does not strengthen a person. This seems clear in Dewey's own statement that in interest the "object[ive] as a moving force *includes the self within it.*" (Dewey and Tufts 1932, 321, 323) Interests, in other words, are motives in which an objective is attained, but by swallowing up the self. Like the ancients, he found the self merging into the object of its caring. This is precisely the point at which Noddings turned the tradition on its head. Noddings found that a person becomes more himself in caring, where Dewey held he was weakened, rather than strengthened, in pursuing his interests.

Twenty years before Dewey made the above comment about interests, he made what are, to the best of my knowledge, his only remarks about concern, which involves much greater commitment and solicitude than does interest. That discussion appeared in 1916 in *Democracy and Education*. There he used the words "interest" and "concern" interchangeably, and he grounded their meaning in his usual analysis of the inseparable but distinguishable functions, intellect and feeling. Rephrasing what he had written in analyzing the reaction to coming unexpectedly upon a bear, he wrote, "The attitude of a participant in the course of affairs is... a double one: there is solicitude, anxiety concerning future consequences, and [there is] a tendency to act to assure better, and avert worse, consequences." The latter aspect of the attitude is referred to by such words as aim, intent, and end; they "emphasize the *results* which are wanted and striven for." The former aspect is denoted by such words as interest, affection, concern, and motivation; they "emphasize the bearing of what is foreseen upon the individual's fortunes, and his active desire to act to secure a possible result." He continued, "We may call the phase of objective foresight intellectual, and the phase of personal concern emotional and volitional." (Dewey 1916, 146, 147) Interest, concern, and affection are aroused, Dewey was asserting, by what is happening to our "fortunes," which, we should point out, are quite different from our "inner welfare." Dewey was writing an educational philosophy, and he rightly selected from among these words the term "interest" to refer to the attitude he had in mind as the key to formal learning.

He was wrong, however, in equating concern and interest. A concerned person is much more heavily invested in a situation than is an interested one. Of two persons, one interested in the progress of fifth graders or the outcome of a vote by the town council and the other concerned about them, we have no difficulty in saying that the latter is *personally* more involved. The person interested in the progress of fifth graders may visit classes, talk to teachers, read educational journals, and make disinterested observations and judgments. When finished, he presumably understands the subject much better and can speak knowledgeably about it. The person concerned with the progress of fifth graders may do many of the same things, but the progress of fifth graders affects him much more intimately. It may be because his child is a fifth grader, he thinks the teaching favors boys over girls or whites over racial minorities, or he believes the curriculum is hurtful to the pupils. For whatever reason, what happens in fifth grade "happens to" him. The "progress," in other words, affects his "inner welfare."

Dewey did not recognize this difference. "Both terms," he concluded, "express engrossment of the self in an object[ive]." (Dewey 1916, 148) They do, but not in the same way or, in most instances, to the same degree. An interested person is more aloof, less committed, than a concerned person. A youngster who is interested in playing baseball may suddenly find the intriguing charms of computing. Where he was so engrossed in playing baseball that he forgot time and missed meals, he now cannot be pulled away from his keyboard. In each case he is engrossed in the project, learning how, improving skills, etc. He may, while interested in playing baseball, also be concerned about whether he will make the team, but that is different. His concern is about his standing as a player, about his relative ability, about himself as a baseball player. In this instance the concern might be considered self-interested, but it need not be selfish. The adult concerned about the education of minority members is engrossed in the same way, and perhaps as deeply, as the youngster trying out for the team. In each experience there is a "return wave" which bonds the activity and its object to the "inner welfare" of the concerned person.

Concern is more basic than interest in determining the quality of life. We often think of self-direction as a management skill in which our expertise in modifying our surroundings is central, as Dewey sometimes seemed to hold in his accounts of problem solving, but the feeling-tone of our experience is much more deeply affected by our self-assessments. Dewey held that intelligence is the tool for improving the quality of life, but it was called into action only when "problems" arose. Its function was to restore equilibrium. This fit in with his notion that organisms maintain equilibrium and, when disturbed, must regain it. The theory was W.B. Cannon's theory of homeostasis, which, again, was a description of physiological processes. The theory was basically that of a control system using feed-back to maintain its functioning within a normal range. A gyroscope maintaining a ship on an even keel offers a ready analogy. While consistent with biological concepts which prevailed at the time, the theory did not explain the increased level of energy of living beings over nonliving or of "higher" animals over less complex organisms. That remained a mystery until it was discovered that there are feed-forward as well as feedback processes.

Personality is such a system of powerful energies. These are most apt to act in a nonlinear fashion when motives of caring and concern exist. These are as natural as those Dewey called attention to, but they are much more apt to speed the spiraling because nurturing is confirmatory and energizing. Those who are nurtured in companionate caring become more competent, more contented, more optimistic, and better able to meet adversity. Such results depend upon the engrossment necessary to companionate caring. There it is the motive which takes the welfare of an "other" into one's own life so that what happens to the other affects one's own welfare. The welfare of the other becomes a part, we might say, of one's own "inner welfare." Caring has as its paradigm case this engrossment in another person, but when the engrossment is in other things and projects and becomes generalized as a feature of character, it is concern.

It is not interest, but concern, which characterizes our deepest feelings and underwrites our strongest motivations. These are exhibited in attitudes which become dominant in the spiraling interadjustments of aims, desires, hopes, judgments, anxieties, and beliefs in the networking consciousness of persons. The strongest reactions we have, the ones which have the greatest impact upon the quality of our lives, are reactions to ourselves and to what we take to be most important. These are found in feelings of pride and guilt, ambition, shame, competence, serenity, anxiety, boredom, envy, feeling touched, feeling moved, feeling good. These are so deepseated and pervasive that they constitute our very stance toward the world. These feelings, attitudes, and assessments reveal, as nothing else can, the cumulative and recursive effects that can accrue in experience which is both self-referential and other-referential. The positive feelings, such as contentment, pride, thankfulness, and love, build personal energies constructively; they serve as feed-forward energies. The negative ones, such as guilt, shame, envy, hatred, anxiety, and boredom, reflect internal conflicts which prevent energies from synergizing. Feelings are both causes and symptoms of where we stand. We can only improve the quality of our lives by becoming more sensitive and responsive persons, but this lays us open to sorrow as well as joy, pain as well as pleasure, rejection as well as nurturing.

# 4.
# THE MATRIX OF RESPONSIBILITY

February 27, 1998

B oth Plato and Nel Noddings tried to describe feelings and the part they play in personality. They differed in the extreme. Plato, a conservative even in his day, thought discipline was the source of social order and depended upon agreement about important central values. Obedience was expected of all but a few, who supposedly were able to discern what was true and good because they controlled their emotions. In that setting, contrary impulses were a threat to social order and it was easy to blame them upon feelings and desires requiring control. By contrast Noddings, describing the people she knew, the people who are emerging in the great transmutation of the modernizing world, saw them earning and showing respect, achieving dignity, and displaying integrity by understanding and nurturing each other as unique persons. What her peers hope for is different, and they expect different things from life and from each other. We don't, as citizens, believe we should blindly obey our political leaders. We don't consider it healthy to suppress our feelings. We don't agree on any one set of beliefs which we think acts as the mainstay for society. We don't accept a society of ranked classes. We have become a pluralistic, democratic, equalitarian society of free people with initiative, strong feelings, and diverse loyalties.

We can now construct the ethics which is implicit in these new beliefs, attitudes, and values. We can begin with the idea of personal responsibility. It differs markedly in our world, and its origin is found in a different source. Responsibility is nurtured rather than assigned, and it is nurtured in caring that is companionate.

## 4.1　THE INTEGRATIVE SELF

Nel Noddings had the benefit of nearly a century of the study of psychology when she described caring. Philosophical psychology took a modern turn in the 1880s and 1890s when John Dewey and William James introduced into the study of personality a perspective we can recognize as similar to the one Francisco Varela developed in biology later on. The position they took, to state it in the most general terms, was that personality is a coalescence of energies which seeks ever greater unity by integrating its components and improving its relationships with neighboring forces. It was Dewey who developed the theory in its greatest detail, paying particular attention to its implications for ethical, social, and educational theory. Personality, as he described it, is an integration of energies seeking to maximize satisfactions. Because, in this formulation, psychological forces gain their strength by increasing their internal unity through handling feelings intelligently, the theory contradicted Plato's view that sound-mindedness arises from the victory of reason in a conflict with emotions; because psychological forces were held to gain in strength also by altering their environment so as to remove impediments to personal satisfaction, the theory contradicted Plato's view that personal concerns must be set aside when they conflict with the way things "really" are. Dewey recognized the self as a dynamical unity seeking to coordinate its feelings and aims as it coordinated its own needs with those of other forces in its environment.

The first step in the turn to this theory of personality was the rejection of the notion that the self is a substance (a soul) somewhere behind and beyond its activity. Dewey and James asserted that the self is psychical events themselves, using biological forces to interact with each other and their surroundings. As Dewey put it during World War I, "There is no ready-made self behind activities. There are complex, unstable, opposing attitudes, habits, impulses which gradually come to terms with one another, and assume a certain consistency of configuration." (Dewey [1922] 1930, 138) The self is that which it had been thought to have. As Gilbert Ryle put it in 1949, the notion that there is something behind experience manipulating it is "the dogma of a ghost in the machine." (Ryle 1949, 15–18) Personality and character are the way in which our habits, hopes, anxieties, memories, sensibilities, and other psychical events interact with each other and their environment.

The "problem" of the self is to integrate these experiences in a satisfying and productive unity. We can therefore call this the integrative theory of personality. It asserts that personality is a process of integration in which a self appears and develops, always seeking further satisfactions. There is not a pre-established form into which the activities that make up the person must fit; they find their fit in their interaction. The process is fluid and open-ended. The events to be integrated are psychical—expectations, memories, desires, inferences, hopes, frustrations, feelings, aims, purposes, pleasures and pains, etc. Each of them is an activity interacting with the others. The pattern of their interactivity is the self, and the energies they use are organic. These interacting events, the self, are unstable and imperfectly unified, and so they are always seeking a better fit in their interactivity, further integration.

Personality is biologically based but a psychical unity achieving both internal integration and mutually beneficial interadjustment with its environment. The integration of the self, then, is a never-ending process in which mental and organic activities never achieve perfect equilibrium, either with each other or forces in the environment. The balance that the self does achieve can be compared to that of a glider, which must maintain a certain speed and adjust to surrounding air flows in order to maintain flight. We can see in this theory of personality an early example of what later came to be thought of as dynamical systems theory.

In an unstable world, human sensitivities detect forces to be taken into account, needs requiring response. Personal energies maintain a dynamical balance by developing appropriate patterns of response. To take a simple example: a newborn infant is often "uncomfortable" because it lacks something. Among the physiological changes indicating such a lack are hunger pangs. The infant's discomfort is manifested by random physical activity, including crying. Balance is restored as food is supplied. The feeling of discomfort and its removal (at this stage) by agencies outside the organism is cyclical. As the cycle is repeated, the infant "learns." Its activity becomes more directed and turns into a signal to the "mothering" agent. Without being conscious yet of being a self, let alone a hungry self, a signaling self, a learning self, a relating self, the infant adjusts to its discomfort by creating a patterned response, or habit, in which the hunger pangs play a constructive role. Physiological balance is restored, but the comfort is that of a person. The signaling, learning, and habit forming are psychical events; they use physiological processes but rearrange and complicate them in a system of pleasures and pains, desires and frustrations, habitual responses, and activating feelings. A self emerges in the process.

Rather than viewing reason and emotions as opposed, as a traditionalist would, Dewey took an entirely different tack, one in which thinking and feelings need to be integrated. Their interadjustive functioning can be shown if we look again at the hungry infant. His hunger pangs are physiological, and he feels uncomfortable. He becomes restless, is fed, repeats the process, and soon learns to focus his efforts upon certain features of his environment in order to relieve his discomfort. The discomfort has been given a meaning, hunger, and his activity has been localized, become a habit. Which came first, the feeling or the thinking? Neither one. The infant identified the feeling by giving it meaning; his response, intelligent or unintelligent, was to the meaning (Dewey 1925, 267). The intellective and affective elements of the experience were interdependent and simultaneous. We cannot respond to the hunger pangs themselves; we can only respond to the hunger we feel, i.e., the meaning we give the pangs (317, 318). Any conflict between feelings and "reason" is already a conflict of meanings. The person involved can resolve the conflict only by finding how to integrate the meanings. Feelings and meanings are inseparable parts of the same experience.

Feelings, events with meanings, register on a scale of need-desire-satisfaction. They seek or register satisfaction. Feelings are activating agents; they set the self in motion. In a conscious organism, a self, the need-desire contained in a feeling detects a discrepancy between the way things are and the way the self would like them to be. It recognizes a problem in a self wanting satisfaction. To feel, thus, is to enter into a problem-solving situation. The same event that, given meaning, constitutes a feeling triggers intellect, the problem-solving facility. In using our intellect, we respond to our desires and needs by developing patterns of response for managing our surroundings. For example, we learn to satisfy our need-desire for food by planting and harvesting crops or taking a job. We learn to satisfy our need-desire for companionship by cultivating friends.

This account reverses that given by Plato of how reason is related to emotion. What is reasonable is what we can do to modify our surroundings so that our desires will be fitted together in the most satisfying pattern we can achieve. To be reasonable is to set upon ways of conducting ourselves—that is, affecting our environment—that best use and channel our emotional energies. We quoted Dewey in section 3.2 above: "Reasonableness is in fact a quality of an effective relationship among desires rather than a thing opposed to desire." (Dewey [1922] 1930, 194): He could not have been more direct and emphatic in his rejection of the idea that reason is an opponent of emotion. "Rationality... is not a force to evoke against impulse and habit. It is the attainment of a working harmony among diverse desires." (196) We don't manage our lives and make them more satisfying by controlling and eliminating our feelings, but by using and coordinating them in patterns of purposeful conduct.

In patterning our responses, developing habits and dispositions, and solving problems, we are becoming more sensitive, more perceptive, more discriminating, and laying ourselves open to more problems, more pleasures and pains, and more ways of doing things. The more our feeling life grows, the more we have to think about; the more successful we are in solving our problems, the wider becomes the range of our interests. We appreciate more as we learn how to use things; we find more uses for them as we appreciate things. "Reason" and "emotion" are not in conflict, and the function of the first is not to "control" or "discipline" the latter. Each flowers with the other. Intellect cultivates feelings, and feelings cultivate interests. Each becomes richer as they become enmeshed.

Healthy development is a process of increasing, complicating, and organizing desires. Problems are dealt with by finding new uses for desires, relating them to other desires in more constructive ways, discovering new desires. The experience of the infant is illustrative. The crying baby, having learned that his discomfort is hunger, makes hunger a part of his life. It is the occasion for feeding, for communicating, entering into a social relationship, becoming dependent upon the food source, gaining control over his surroundings, developing competence and confidence, trusting another, giving and gaining affection, bonding with another, appreciating food and affection, and gaining a sense of self. The habits have created new sensitivities, new connections, new satisfactions, new competencies, new forms of response. Furthermore, these are not separate achievements. They grow together, have an impact on each other, interrelate. They become characteristic patterns of activity and qualities of the emerging person. Since feelings are meanings given to events, growth means discovering new meanings and new relationships of meanings. This does not mean that all feelings are desirable, but it does mean that undesirable ones can only be displaced by other, more rewarding feelings. They gain or lose their power as they are related to other desires. What we seek—happiness, health, maturity, integration, fulfillment, whatever you may call it—is a life of deeper feelings and improved ways of managing affairs so that satisfactions are more numerous, more prolonged, and more closely related.

We are our integration of our needs and desires and satisfactions in patterns of response dealing with them. Our dispositions are characteristic ways of responding—forthrightly or cunningly, persistently or quixotically, fearlessly or cautiously, warmly or with reserve, questioningly or dogmatically—and these characteristic modes of conduct encompass many more specific reactions. We call them traits of personality, or even virtues or vices, because they truly characterize a person—they describe his character. In forming habits, then, we are creating our own tendencies. Our habits reflect the choices we have made, and choices are decisions we make about what is worthwhile. What we do habitually is what we think it sensible to do. We have made a decision about what ways of going about things are satisfying and reasonable.

Our habits, dispositions, and characteristics sensitize us in a specific way. "Each habit demands appropriate conditions for its exercise and when habits are numerous and complex, as with the human organism, to find these conditions involves search and experimentation." (Dewey 1925, 281) In our search and experimentation we are trying to satisfy ourselves, and our feelings register our reaction to what we come upon. Dewey referred to feelings as a "running commentary of likes and dislikes, attractions and disdains, joys and sorrows." (Dewey [1922] 1930, 201) The "meaning" we give an incident is assigned on the basis of what we know and want. When we react negatively, our feeling is one of dissatisfaction, and therefore suggests strongly that there is something important that remains to be done. We integrate our experience by enlarging the range of our desires to take into account these unsatisfied desires. Feelings are stimulants: they reveal a conflict between the way we do things and the outcomes we want, between our habits and our desires, and thus cause us to re-evaluate what we are doing.

What we have available with which to work out a satisfying resolution of conflicting aims and desires are the patterns of conduct we have already formed, but not all dispositions are equally helpful. Dogmatism, blind obedience, self-satisfaction, anxiety, self-pity, and fanaticism are all examples of attitudes that discourage adventuresomeness and resourcefulness, impartial examination of possibilities, and responsiveness to the great variety in experience. They tend to narrow one's perspective, deaden one's sensitivities, and inhibit one's initiative. They cause one to become "defensive," to reject new ideas and ways of doing things, to shy away from risks. People in whom these attitudes dominate are "set in their ways." For them habits are forms of confinement. The habits may be unpleasant, as anxiety and self-pity are, or comforting, as dogmatism and self-satisfaction are, but they adopt these patterns of response in order to protect themselves. They hang on to what they have, afraid of what lies ahead of them. They are protecting themselves against growth, the broadening of interests, the cultivation of tastes, unknown adventures and pleasures.

Attitudes, habits, and valuations are liberating, however, if they prepare us to recognize, appreciate, and use novelties. Intelligence is just this forward-looking stance. Intelligent ways of dealing with life are achieved by "fostering the impulses and habits which experience has shown to make us sensitive, generous, imaginative, impartial in perceiving the tendency of our inchoate dawning activities." (Dewey [1922] 1930, 207) These are the ones that are most important to us as we evaluate our situation, imagine options for action, and foresee their outcomes. Acting intelligently is like gardening, in which planting, pruning, fertilizing, and watering are essential. Weeding is also helpful, but it is incidental. Weed control is not done for its own sake, but to get rid of obstacles to the healthy growth of the desired plants. In the same way, we inhibit some desires, not for the sake of self-discipline, but to clear the way for other dispositions and desires. It is the cultivation of desires, the development of needs, that opens us to experience.

We live with the dispositions we cultivate; we cultivate the impulses that seem to promise the most satisfying life. We become well integrated as pleasures and desires are cultivated, multiplied, broadened, and built into dispositions, tendencies, and personal characteristics that incorporate inquisitiveness, imagination, innovation, impartiality, and discrimination. This account is diametrically opposed to the classical account of personality. One who seeks simply to discipline his desires defends his present aims and sentiments as the final ones; learning, greater sensitivity, responsiveness to a broader range of experience are closed to him. One who makes inquisitiveness, imagination, and sensitivity habitual finds new desires and needs all the time. One cultivates; the other inhibits. One manages life by cultivating his tastes, impulses, and sensibilities; the other manages his by seeking control over himself.

The cultivation of habits, impulses, and dispositions is not a process that goes on simply within an individual, for these events and characteristics are forms of interaction between the self and its surroundings. "Attitudes, dispositions and their kin.... are always *of, from, toward,* situations and things." (Dewey 1925, 238) In fact, the things and objects which constitute our environment are constructions. We discern them as such because, as such, they are instrumental to our attempts to solve whatever problem confronts us. We single them out from our surroundings because we are able to satisfy our important desire by doing so.

Thus, for example, we identify the apple because it satisfies our hunger. It serves as a means to the end which animates us, and the end is given importance because we are hungry. The apple is means-end. While we are hungry and have nothing to eat, it is end, something sought; once discovered and recognized as nutritious, it is means. The hunger is also means-end. As felt experience, it is an end to be satisfied; its satisfaction is means to maintain our health. Our experience is a series of objectives, ends-in-view and objects singled out as ends (objectives), that is, means to attain those ends. Experience is a means-end continuum. We use our intelligence to make the valuations which distinguish what is important and what can be the instrumentalities for achieving what is important. Since what is important is what will remove our dissatisfactions with the way things are, intelligence is devoted to making our experience more satisfying.

This account had several advantages. First of all, it built upon Dewey's discovery that feelings and ideas are just two aspects of the same experience, namely, giving meaning to events. Further, it was a corollary of his description of the self as a grouping of feelings, habits, valuations, meanings, tensions, and impulses. The identification of ends and means was an activity coordinating these psychical events. Thus it got away from the "ghost in the machine," the substantive self "behind" psychical events and made the self a natural process coordinating biological energies. And finally, combining these two features, it laid the groundwork for finding that the function of intelligence is the coordination of the desires which grow out of the frustrations and dissatisfactions that are crystallized in problematic situations. Problems are the intellective formulations of these unsatisfied desires.

There were, however, two difficulties implicit in the account. The first was voiced by a number of critics. How do we know which desires should be satified? While it seems entirely reasonable to believe that what we find problematic, distressing, a source of dissatisfaction, is the blocking of a desire, we can readily identify desires which should be inhibited. Dewey's account, while giving a natural account of the origin of value, seemed unsatisfying as an account of the way in which we can and should judge among them. The second difficulty becomes apparent when we ask how the desires of one person are to be related to the desires, and therefore the needs, of others. In satisfying one's own desires, the needs of others and of society considered as a whole seem to be disregarded. What is the relationship of society to selves treated as problem-solving agents when problem solving is itself seen as the maximization of personal satisfactions? To formulate the two objections in their common element: Dewey did not offer an adequate account of the regulative function by which intelligence can satisfy the needs and aims of either society or the agent himself.

In examining the way in which Dewey dealt with these two problems, we will find that, despite the great advances he made, he was himself constrained by his retention of elements of the classical tradition. Considered by his critics to have gone too far, he had not gone far enough. The result was that he was unable to provide a standard for either personal development or social responsibility within the natural setting he described so presciently. He, too, like Adam Smith and Darwin, described a process but failed to discover the dynamic at work. In his case, because he was concerned with ethical life with its choices, principles, and satisfactions, his philosophy gave no guidance for central questions and, in fact, fostered antisocial tendencies. In cultivating certain dispositions and inhibiting or reconstructing others, we are altering our sensitivities and our responsiveness to the many kinds of events that impinge upon us. Thus personal satisfaction, though it suggests (because of our inherited psychology) a self-interested motivation, is necessarily a matter of satisfying relationships with forces that lie beyond us.

Chief among these are other people, and particularly those most important to us. Personal satisfaction is wrapped up with relationships that are mutually sustaining. There is no "natural" and inevitable conflict between people because people do not have "base" instinctual drives that are opposed to intelligent living; their needs become destructive and immoral only when they are not integrated with other aims and desires in ways that contribute to further satisfactions. An important aspect of managing life intelligently lies in the selective cultivation of attitudes, habits, feelings, and aims that strengthen mutually sustaining relationships at the expense of destructive ones. Just as reasonableness is a disposition developed out of "flickering impulses," so also are dispositions that strengthen personal relationships— to be sympathetic, open, nurturing, and understanding.

The claims of the integrative theory of personality turn out to be nothing more than assertions that personality operates in the same way all of nature does. A person is a self-maintaining, self-directing swirl of energies. There is no self behind these interadjusting energies, any more than there is an atom behind interadjusting protons, neutrons, and electrons or a tornado behind the swirling winds interadjusting to the earth's coriolis effect or a "life principle" behind the molecular interadjustments of an organism. Persons are integrative-relational energy systems. Personality is integrative and relational.

The integrative theory of personality denied the splits between reason and emotion, self and others, that plagued classical views. It was a remarkable achievement because it cut so deeply into the assumptions about personality that had been accepted for so long. It was highly persuasive and had great influence for a time; clearly it resonated with twentieth-century yearnings. In the end, however, it came under severe criticism. It was dismissed by man as overly "permissive." The criticism contained the reaction of a culture brought up to believe that natural tendencies are dangerous and must be brought under control. The cultivation of feelings and interests sounded all too much like aiding and abetting the forces of evil.

Looking back, we can see what was wrong. Two things were lacking. First, the then current and still dominant theory of nature was mechanistic and atomistic. It featured a picture of reality in which individuals maintaining and directing themselves by relating to other autonomous individuals in mutually beneficial arrangements were anachronisms. The integrative self pictured by Dewey and others was an anomaly, unnatural. That difficulty has been alleviated somewhat by the development of dynamical systems theory. As a result, it is possible to see personality, and specifically feelings and thoughtfulness, in a more dynamical light. Second, Dewey was unable to identify the feeling which might generate attitudes and motives that would bring people seeking fulfillment together in responsible social arrangements. For Dewey it was mostly upsetting feelings which triggered reactions. Although near the end of his career he considered the nature of appreciation and other "consummatory" experiences, his primary concern was always with problems and problem solving. In his picture of problem solving, people were addressing disturbing feelings and regaining a state of relative equilibrium by altering the situation that aroused the feelings. Intelligent activity, on this model, was much like the feedback provided by control mechanisms; it restored equilibrium. The theory of dynamical systems teaches us, however, that systems maintaining themselves depend upon processes that feed upon themselves and so sustain, or even increase, their energy levels. Dealing with "problems" and "frustrations" is necessary, but hardly energizing. What is needed is a source of feed forward that creates synergies.

## 4.2    THE GENERATIVE SELF

This was the remarkable achievement of Nel Noddings. As a teacher and educational philosopher she was strongly influenced by Dewey, but she was sensitive enough to personal relationships that she could not be confined by his stress upon the intellective elements of personality integration. In her experience personal relationships originate in a sensitive reception of the feelings of another and an emotional engrossment in their cares and concerns. We have described the process in detail. It constituted an important amendment and improvement of Dewey's theory of personality.

Feelings and intelligence are closely related, and their healthy relationship is one of mutual interadjustments and support. But feelings are more directly animating; they have greater force and are more easily aroused. In finding their arousal to be the source of caring, Noddings was making personality itself more dynamic. The integration of personality, she saw, required more than the removal of dissatisfactions and a return to equilibrium; it consisted in creating new and broader satisfactions, the preservation of a dynamical instability. Dewey had made growth the central concept of healthy living; Nodding described the dynamic by which it occurs. She was converting the integrative theory of personality into a generative theory of personality.

Dewey, like Adam Smith and Darwin, had formulated a theory which correctly described what went on but did not identify the source of the energy at work. His contribution was momentous. He found that personality development is the integration of feelings and aims, and neither feelings nor aims are fixed. Desirable aims, he insisted, are not those satisfied by contemplating what exists but by intelligently changing it; thus intelligence replaced reason. Similarly with feelings: they are not innate and obstructive, but meanings given events and therefore subject to intelligent cultivation, reform, and use. But he never was able to show how the cultivation, reform, and use of feelings could lead to responsible living. Although sharing and community participation were always primary values for him and intelligent living was essential to them, he never showed how feelings contributed to them. He thus left unanswered the question why what is satisfying to us must be worthwhile.

We can only answer this question if we understand persons to be seeking a more meaningful and satisfying existence by networking with other persons. To hold this is to recognize that the search is never-ending, that there are always more and richer satisfactions, more and deeper meanings to be discovered and achieved. Persons are developing: their problem is not to identify "the good" but to create a life which is more satisfying because they are more understanding.

This is the quest which is ethical. It takes place in nature, and it consists in developments that take place in the one on quest. It proceeds by mobilizing energies and insights. It doesn't deal with a separate realm of energies and insights, but merely the improvement and better direction of all our energies and insights. Let us turn to the way in which companionate caring cultivates the energies and insights which are best able to help people seek and create lives which are satisfying and worthwhile. We can begin at the beginning. We start out as "a bundle of nerves" being cared-for. We are sensitive and responsive, and we are in the arms of others who are sensitive and responsive. Our progress toward personhood proceeds as the sensitivities and responses of those who cherish us are fine-tuned to our own sensitivities and responses. The specifics of caring—fondling, caressing, cooing, rocking, etc.—are so important that the other, more obvious necessities, such as air, food, water, and rest, cannot serve their purpose in our growth unless accompanied by them. Physical, emotional, and social development are all contingent upon and outgrowths of caring offered personally; its implications for moral development are very great at every stage of our development.

Although we are not conscious of being cherished at the beginning, since we have no basis for judging and no self to do the judging, we soon become dimly aware. We begin as a "me." It appears in experiences such as "s/he rocks me," "s/he dries me," "s/he feeds me," "s/he comes when s/he hears me cry." There is only a "me"; there is no "I" yet. "Me" is an object, taken care of, being served. Me's actions at this stage are largely reflexive; they require no decision. Me sleeps, wiggles, cries, sucks, pees, and burps. These actions may cause responses on the part of a loving other, but they don't need me's thought. Me is a creation of others and in their care. "I" will appear out of me only as a product of their care.

As "I" emerge and take in the situation, I correctly perceive that things are done for me lovingly in response to my recognized needs. I am the object of caring and services. What is good or bad, in this initial world, is what does or does not respond warmly and effectively to my needs. Note that this initial perception is dual: it is aware both of the services being provided and the caring being lavished. Both are important, but how I think they are related is what is essential and this depends upon what kind of caring I am receiving. From the beginning the ones cared-for are as responsive to being cherished as they are to receiving services. They are sensitive enough to distinguish loving care from routine care, caring others from service providers. If the ones-caring offer their care companionately, the ones cared-for develop a self that reflects this fact. If not, they take a different path.

The ones-caring may be indifferent in their caring or unsuccessful in completing it, and one of the most common ways of failing, we can now see, is to treat the caring as a routine, that is to say, to fail to receive the one cherished. This is commonly done by people who think caring means applying rules to those they care for. If they do that, however, they may well be satisfying the needs and wants of their charges, but they are not displaying the understanding that comes only through receiving another. The ones cared-for then adopt the standard implied by their nannies' treatment: they define themselves in terms of their needs and wants and value others according to their success in satisfying them. It is no wonder, since this happens all too frequently, that "enlightened self-interest" is a popular ethical theory. It has an obvious naturalness to it, for it correctly describes what has happened to many people. Their others—to oversimply differences that are nearly always of degree rather than of kind—have been service providers rather than ones-caring, and as a result they define themselves as deserving recipients of services and goods and value others chiefly as means to that end. They have been led quite naturally by the treatment they have received to a theory of value that demands of them only conduct arranged so as to maximize their benefits and minimize their repayments. Their moral development has been subverted to a prudent attempt to manage situations so as to serve their selfish interests. They define themselves as what they are getting rather than what they are becoming.

When, however, the services are an expression of companionate caring, the ones cared-for receive both the services and the loving care and cannot separate them from each other. The ones-caring are offering their love, and the service is only the vehicle of that love. The caring is an attitude of regard for the one cared-for as an other who is independent of the one-caring's own needs. From the very beginning, the ones-caring treat the cared-for as a person who has needs and wants and who is sensitive and responsive to them. They respond to the cared-for as a person as well as to his needs, and, in so doing, they act to create a person. His self does not yet exist; it is a persona bestowed upon him. The imagined self is quite specific, and it evolves rapidly as the ones-caring modify their attitudes and actions to take into account his responses. The cared-for adjusts to act the role he is given; it is that of a specific *conferred* self (Norton 1991, 161-2). The ones-caring enter into an interadjustive relationship with the one cared-for, and his responses, as he begins to identify himself as a participant in their interactions, are both contributions to the community so created and elements of his self-definition.

The self that emerges in such caring contains a

self-evaluation. The caring others communicate to the cared-for their sense of his worth; it is contained in the self they confer on him. The cared-for accepts the conferred self proudly because it expresses the pride the ones-caring feel in him. His worth is a prominent and essential feature of the self he is originally given and accepts. It is out of this original imputed worth that all the values he can subsequently realize, all the virtues he can later achieve, are born. Every self, no matter at what stage of development it may be, is also a self-in-process-of-becoming. It may seem mysterious that people are never entirely satisfied with what they are and are always trying to become something more, but now we can see why this is so. In this most natural transfer, loving others wrap their dreams of a worthy person and a satisfying life in the self they confer upon the one they cherish. From the outset the dream is as real as the actuality and a part of it; the self we have conferred upon us contains our worth. From the very beginning, we have the urge to improve the quality of our life and our self. And we get this urge from those who confer our self upon us in the first place, those who cherish us.

This incompleteness of human beings, always combined with an almost ineradicable striving to gain greater satisfaction and become more worthwhile, has been noted by others, but no adequate explanation for it has been given. Carl Rogers, for example, when he stripped down counseling so that it was a non-directive therapy which left improvement pretty much in the hands of the client, found there was a tendency in his clients to overcome their neurotic deficiencies. He described it as very similar to the tendency of the physical organism to heal wounds or counter infections. He could not explain it and so suggested that there might be some natural healing force at work, an innate tendency of the organism (Rogers 1961, 194), but the simplest explanation is that this is the primal learning of people whose initial utter dependency places their sensitivity and responsiveness in the hands of others who introduce them into a community of caring. Their drive to improve themselves and the quality of their lives is not organic, but personal, a product of caring.

## 4.3 THE NATURAL HISTORY OF "I MUST"

When we described natural caring as it was experienced by the one-caring, we noted that at the center of the experience was an "I must" that activated his response to the one cherished. For him this was felt as a need he had to satisfy. That need was not present at birth, but an emergent in socializing development. We can now trace its origins in the experience of one being cherished. It is he who senses the attitude of the one who cares for him and recognizes the evaluation contained in it. He feels that he is worth the attention, the regard, because the ones who constitute his whole experience give his welfare such high priority. But the caring must be companionate if it is to have this effect. The "I must" may be analyzed—but not separated—into the following elements: (1) I, caring, (2) must do something (3) in response to your need (4) to help you deal with it.

The caring others approach a newborn with this attitude, but they implement the attitude in a much different way than they do in a relationship with a more fully developed person. In a caring relationship between adults, we noted, the one-caring had to respect the autonomy of the one cherished. He did not decide how to intervene without consulting the cared-for, and his support was limited to what the cared-for would accept from him (as well as what he could offer genuinely). Here, however, he is much more activist, for the cherished other does not yet have a self of his own. Not being able to give advice to him, the one-caring must imagine what troubles him and provide the service that will deal with its cause. This merges the third and fourth elements of the reaction. What would be obtrusive for a cared-for who is a clearly defined person is now a necessary action. The caring person is at this stage a caretaker; he is dealing with a helpless but needful object. Not yet a self, the infant is utterly dependent. He must be helped. At first he must be fed, cuddled, and changed; later he must have his shoe laces tied, be taught games and manners. Yet, even at this stage, his otherness must also be respected. Part of the task of the ones-caring is to meet the infant's needs, and part of it is to activate his self so he will not remain dependent. The two functions are parts of the same task, and each can be done successfully only when combined with the other. The ones-caring can only succeed by conferring a self upon the one cared-for before he has one and providing their services to this imputed self.

How they treat the self they confer is crucial to its development. They give substance to the conferred self by assigning it a role. The role is very simple at first and much coaching is needed. The role is that of a happy person, and so the infant is encouraged to laugh and feel pleasures. It is that of a much loved person, and so affection is lavished upon him and elaborately expressed. It is that of a competent person, and so he is given simple tasks he can perform well. It is that of a responsive person, and so his responses are elicited by cuddling and caressing him and tossing him in the air. It is that of an adventurous person, and so he is given tasks that call for the use of new skills. It is that of a responsible person, and so he is given simple duties. He grows into his role and, treated always as a person who is comfortable in his role, he becomes the self for whom the "part" is natural. The self has been conferred upon him, and he has accepted it.

The self becomes more firmly ensconced and more clearly defined as the caring others accept, affirm, and nurture him. They build upon these early expectations and achievements in this way, and the one cared-for, using their acceptance and affirmation, ventures forth on his own. He comes to recognize himself as an other, as a person with particular qualities and competences, specific strengths and weaknesses. Increasingly, as he asserts himself, the caring others come to distinguish the third and fourth elements of caring. More and more the ones-caring respond to the emerging selfhood of their cared-for: increasingly they direct their caring to him and leave it up to him to define his needs and solve his problems. They stand ready, but as others. Their primary attitude is one of support for him. They can respond to pleas for help; they can offer their services, but they can no longer solve his problems.

How do they prepare him for the risks he must take as he tries to assert his conferred self? They give him duties and some simple rules by which he can fulfill them. They assign duties by offering a "You must" to him. They are recognizing that the cherished other must accept the conferred self, and that this requires learning; acceptance cannot be total at first. They therefore offer their "I must" to the cared-for in the form of a "You must."

The "I must" they feel has a content which specifies what they think he must do to satisfy his needs and fulfill the role of the self they have conferred. As he becomes capable of acting on his own behalf, they pass on to him the responsibility for doing what they think is required. They are defining the self they have conferred, and at the same time they are offering him a chance to make it his own. By accepting the gift, the cared-for asserts his independence of the ones caring by demonstrating that he no longer needs their assistance in performing the functions of the conferred self. He thus transfers to himself the regulative function of the "I must" and takes a step toward assuming the self that has been conferred upon him.

There is no rebellion in this act if the transfer is offered generously and as soon as the cared-for is ready to assume the obligation. It is the most natural thing in the world. It is also, however, crucial to the moral development of the cared-for, for in this way the ones-caring wean him away from the erroneous perception that he is properly only the recipient of services and gifts. They are helping him to find out, to define, who he is. They are also allowing him to enter into their community. By offering him this access, they are taking a very important step in both his psychosocial and his moral development. They are defining his self as a constituent part of their community and their community as a network of persons that includes him. In a networking psychosocial reality, personality and society, character and community, are interadjustive and collaborative. In classical theory there has been much debate about which comes first, presumably because that one is determinative of the other, but in networks causation is pulsing, spiraling.

The community is one of give and take if it is caring. The "elders," in caring, are responding to the needs of the newcomers. But, at the same time, the newcomers are assuming assigned duties in roles that call upon them to discover the complexities of a promising future. Each role has simple duties, and these duties are important both as responses to the needs of others and as clues to the personal qualities of the character who plays the role.

That character is already roughly sketched out in the expectations of those who care, which are made clear in the assigned duties. The duties help to define the emerging self that is being conferred upon the cared-for. They are his obligations because they are the natural functions of the person who has the worth imputed to him. They are given proudly by the loving others who envision this worth as his promise, and they are accepted with pride because the cared-for accepts this loving assessment. The duties are essential aspects of the dream that is offered as a gift by the ones-caring and that is ultimately shared by the one cared-for. They are functions of the role-playing through which he is developing his self.

The community of caring others is also defined in these duties. The duties are not only the obligations of the cared-for, but also obligations he has toward others. The community, in defining the duties sensitively, invites the newly forming person to emerge as one performing services as well as playing a role. By accepting the role and carrying out its functions, he becomes a peer in the community. The duties are minor by comparison with those of others, but this does not matter. In caring, it is the achievement of worth that is sought, and achievement of the worth appropriate to childhood is as meritorious for a child as the achievement of worth appropriate to adulthood is for an adult. A caring community respects the uniqueness of the worth of each by recognizing its equal importance for the further development of its bearer. The value of the contribution to the community, by comparison with this consideration, is less important. Thus the child enters a community in which judgments of relative value are subordinate to the nurturing potency of caring.

By its receptive attitude the community serves to elicit ever greater degrees of mastery in each of its members. Still, the learning has to be staged carefully. The load assigned the young must involve tasks that can be performed successfully, so they can become confident and competent as they meet challenges, but it must also test their capacity, so they come to accept challenges as a part of their lives and growth as natural. If the assigned duties serve these functions, the cared-for finds the basis for accepting them and taking pride in performing them as he fits into his conferred self. In carrying out his obligations, he defines himself as something more than a dependent and finds reason to think the worth that others have found in him—and that has led to the specific duties assigned to him—are indeed real possibilities for him. Properly assigned, the tasks and duties both define the individuality that he must display in his own growth and open up to him the community in which it can be completed.


## 4.4   DUTIES AND OBLIGATIONS

Ultimately the cared-for becomes eager to play the role as his own, to assert his own individuality. Those who cherish him find this out quickly, for they come to symbolize for him the dependency he wants to escape. But they also remain as mentors, loving others, and supports for the new self he is trying to define for himself. The "problems" of parents reflect the struggle their child has to grow up. The parents who succeed—the most loving ones who have instilled a strong sense of self in their child—are the ones who may feel most under siege. The worth they have inculcated in him is very real to him, and he is secure in feeling it is his future; he is impatient to realize it. They have to walk a narrow line between smothering his impulses for growth and leaving him without adequate support and guidance. For them, the rule is only that there is no rule to follow. They can only do their best to be sensitive to rapid changes and responsive to his emerging needs.

For the child, however, rules have a part to play. The "You must" he has accepted serves as a crutch as he tries out the self conferred upon him. He is at risk, and he is fearful. He makes mistakes and experiences failures. But he also has adventures and triumphs. He wants to go further, do more, take charge, and he is encouraged to do so as he meets success. But this does not always happen, and so he needs support. His adventuresomeness can be smothered if the rules prevent his experimentation and they can cause failure if they demand too much of him. They must be nurturing, i.e., they must accept him as he is and affirm him as he can become. At an early age, both what he can do and what he can learn to do change rapidly, and rules need to change to reflect this.

As long as rules call for conduct that allows him to demonstrate the worth he has at this stage of his development and as long as they are related to functions that allow him to enter into the support network of the community, they serve a constructive purpose. These conditions, however, are essential, and they can be met only if the ones-caring permit the cared-for to become the self they are conferring upon him by permitting him to take charge of the responses by which he meets his constantly changing needs. If they do this, the duties and the rules by which they are enforced can become his. The "You must" that was offered him can be accepted, to become his "I must." The duties have then been accepted because he has begun to see himself as possessing the worth that others have seen in him, and he is beginning to realize that worth by performing the functions entailed in it. Thus, as the ones-caring move from the provision of services to the supportive role of caring others, they allow the cared-for to become a one-caring, also. This is, of course, just what they hoped for, but they still may find it difficult to withdraw because they know the risks he faces and fear his failure. Yet, if they do not draw back at this stage, they impede his progress by preventing his self-assertion and transferring their fears to him. To the extent caring others do not recognize this demand placed upon their caring and so continue to assume the feeling-defining, response-formulating, decision-making functions of the one they care for, they intrude upon and weaken essential self-defining functions that he must use to develop in a healthy fashion.

This is just another way of saying what we have made clear previously, namely, that nurturing is a form of personal support, not a gift or loan. A gardener knows that he can plant the seeds and provide favorable conditions for growth, but he cannot influence what kind of flower grows from them. Similarly, caring others must have confidence in the worth they have conferred upon their cared-for and the formative role it can play in his development. This does not always happen. Sometimes rules are to be followed "because I say so" or because "parents know best," but, to the extent the rules are detached from the duties and the vision of a particular responsible person, they lose their raison d'être for the child and become confining rather than freeing in their effect. The cared-for may conform to the rule and be dutiful, but the "You must" becomes for him an "I ought to." He accepts it, but as an imposition.

This disconnection of rules from their justification in the necessities of growth guided by caring is all too common. In fact, rules are generally used as a short-cut. They are placed upon the child as a demand by the community, and the parents or their surrogates serve only as messengers and enforcers. Then rules serve to stifle growth rather than encourage it. In such circumstances, the child subordinates himself to the demands of the group when he acts in accordance with the rules; when he violates the rules, he is asserting himself against the rigid controls of a constraining social group. In this instance, also, parents have "problems" with their children. On the surface their problems do not seem all that different from those experienced by parents whose caring is completed in their children, but they are enormous. Now the rules take center stage, replacing the worth there. The rebel is now trying to assert himself by declaring his freedom from social controls rather than by discovering how to demonstrate his worth in a caring community. When children are seeking their individuality, one may do so within the community and the other outside his group.

Note carefully the language used here. The latter

child is responding to a social group, not a community. For him there is no community, only a group legislating for its members. He has received the rules, but those enforcing the rules are not receiving his feelings and the caring is not completed in him. As a result, the duties do not appear to him as the natural functions of the person he is potentially, a person with worth; they remain the teachings of others. He perceives the "You must" of others as his "I ought to." This is acceptance combined with rejection. He realizes he is expected to conform, but he internalizes no reason to do so. He is denying himself when he obeys. He does not trust others as a cared-for does the ones who cherish him, and their teachings remain external to his emotional commitment. If he performs the duties, he does so to please the others. It is not their caring he is responding to, but their power. This is social interaction, but it is power-driven. The relationships are not nurturing, but prudential. Changes are not developmental, but reactive, the self-seeking exchanges of isolates. And the rules by which the duties are carried out and enforced are external, imposed.

A community is joined in a much different way: it does not operate by rules: it is caring, and caring can never be expressed simply by following a rule. It may be expressed by offering a rule the cared-for can follow, but this offer is caring only if it is understood as temporary and as a means to an end, that is to say, serving as guidance for those who are as yet unable to define their own course. Both its temporary quality and its status as a means are made clear by relating the rule to the still-developing person who will not need such external guidance later. Because personal needs are developmental, rules are temporary expedients of a selfhood that is emerging as self-initiating and self-regulating. They will be cast off when they are no longer needed.

To think of caring as the inculcation of rules or to express one's caring merely by imposing rules upon the cared-for is to define good as obedience to rules and virtue as pleasing others. Here, of course, we are back in the tradition-bound society described by Plato, where virtue required agreement about what is right. The dynamism of caring does not exist there; it has been smothered by rules.

For many, moral conduct is nothing more than obeying the rules that define what is right, but rules, in the nature of the case, cannot constitute a satisfactory ethics. Ethics is a more creative process: it consists of efforts to achieve personal worth. The "I must" is an essential aspect of a being who will forever be incomplete and striving to achieve greater worth, but it must change to serve its purpose.

## 4.5   From Duties to Responsibilities

The distinction between the "I must" and the "I ought to" is basic. The former is a choice, the latter an imposition. The difference lies largely in the extent to which the ones-caring succeed in communicating to their cared-fors the worth they are imputing to them. When the duty is accepted as a natural feature of that worth, it is chosen. When the worth is not clear to the cared-for, the duty is a restraint.

Given a companionately caring environment, a child can be secure in his worth from the beginning. He has been accepted for what he is but also affirmed in what he can become, and so he sees himself as a person-in-process-of-becoming. Wanting to improve the quality of his life, he identifies it as a primary concern and moves to take charge of it, one aspect at a time. If he cannot take charge, as is often the case when the duties have been assigned him without being related to a self which has worth, he does what is expected of him (or rebels at doing it), plays a role, performs functions, carries out duties. But the role is assigned, the values are borrowed, and the duties are formal. The sense of obligation, of necessity, is directed at others. He pleases himself by pleasing others. This is entirely proper in a life that is not yet one's own. In childhood it is normal: the only possible one, in fact, for a child has not yet chosen who he will be. He is still dreaming of "who he will be when he grows up."

If this dutiful life becomes an end in itself, it can have tragic consequences. Then the imposed duties are generalized, stereotyped. This may happen if those in charge have their own idea of what the one cared-for should be like. If this is the case, they do not receive his feelings and build upon them. They are not engrossed sufficiently to notice just what is troubling the child or what gives him joy; they already have an idea what should be troubling or joyful, and they call upon the cared-for to live according to these idealized standards. They offer duties and obligations that have not been tailored specifically to him. They do not build on his particular competences, recognize his particular frailties and limitations, or use his budding aspirations. They are customized duties and obligations, and they fit poorly. They embody the values of the ones caring rather than the worth of the one cared-for. Anyone is sensitive enough to see when he is not the real object of attention and concern, and his responsiveness is stunted. What he sees in those around him is a blurred image of who he is and should be because they are projecting a stereotyped persona upon him and are not accepting him as he is. They cannot affirm his future self because it can only grow out of the present self they have not received and accepted. Since the vision they have for him is not a development specifically out of his present self, he can only see himself as a failure.

He can, however, recognize his duties and responsibilities. These take on greater importance in his relationships with others as the lack of their engrossment distances them from him, and he perceives the duties and rules he has been given as absolute and inflexible. They are not justified by his vision of who he wants to be, and so he must accept them literally. They have no special application to him. What is expected of him is expected also of everyone else, and so it makes no great difference whether the duties are carried out by him or by someone else. If he doesn't do them, perhaps someone else will. He has become fungible. Anyone else can replace him. And so he has no sense of his own worth, which must be specific to him and envision values that only he can create.

He is confined to a world of rules, and there is nothing unique about him. He has entered into a framework of understanding and expectation in which he can carry out his obligations only by denying his own uniqueness. He can only feel good about himself and gain the approval of others if he follows rules he cannot justify. If, recognizing that he is somehow demeaning himself, he rebels, he gains the enmity or disapproval of others. If, currying favor, he does what he has been told, he becomes alienated from his own feelings. He is bound to be resentful, for he can see that what is expected of him is no more directly related to his experience than is what he receives from others. His tragedy is personal. His relationships with others are deadened, and he is depersonalized.

It is entirely different for one introduced into a caring community. For him the rules and duties have a constructive meaning. By accepting them he can participate in the community and demonstrate in this way his distinctive qualities. Others, sensitive to his needs—for understanding, recognition, and appreciation, as well as guidance and support—respond to him as unique. He in turn discovers their needs and their uniqueness and tailors his responses to them. Every step makes the next more natural. Each response, designed to meet a specific need in another, elicits a reinforcing response. He has entered upon a spiral of fulfillment in which sensitivity and response resonate. He is developing and strengthening his own individuality in a process that calls for more and more nurturing from him and elicits more and more nurturing from others. The community is strengthened as his individuality becomes more pronounced. He has entered into a feed-forward loop which uses community to reinforce individuality and individuality to reinforce community.

A member of a caring community discovers himself in that community. His vision of who he is and can be becomes clearer as he relates to others in nurturing ways and as he takes charge of his life to cope with his problems. He may or may not agree with his "elders" in the community about what qualities are those he should assume and what abilities he should cultivate in himself, but the others see those as questions he ultimately must answer for himself. They therefore provide understanding rather than insist upon agreement. Step by step they grant him the autonomy he craves, recognizing that it is the natural flowering of the worth they have lovingly inserted in the self they have conferred upon him. His "I must" becomes grounded in his own desires, and it is much more likely to contain large elements of the "You must" they conferred just because he is free to make the decision himself. It is intrusion and repression that causes rebellion. Caring that accepts and affirms the otherness and the autonomy of the cared-for nurtures a more natural and humane reaction.

Those who are objects of such caring grasp their autonomy, and refuse to accept duties and obligations simply because they are assigned to them by others. We have called these assigned functions duties or obligations for a reason. The words connote something imposed, and eventually we must resent being imposed upon in this way. The duties or obligations imposed upon us by others contrast with the responsibilities we accept as the moral necessities of the person we "must" be. For the latter, the word "responsibility" becomes appropriate because then the "I must" is self-generated rather than borrowed or assigned. The word "responsibility" derives from the same word as "response." A responsibility is a response expressing personal concern. It is self-initiated. It grows out of the sensitivities of an engrossed person; the self has become enlarged and activated in that engrossment and the responsibility is morally necessary to the fulfillment of that larger self.

The distinction between a responsibility and an obligation or duty is, then, nothing other than the difference between the "I must," the sense of oughtness in a person who has discovered his worth, and the "I ought to," the sense of oughtness in one who has not. A responsibility is accepted as following from one's choice of the person he is to be and so as a feature of the life that person must live. An obligation or duty is a sense of oughtness not so anchored, but rather a sense of obligation accepted as a part of a self dependent upon others for approval.

Moving from obligations to responsibilities is a key step in personal, social, and moral development. It is common to think of the urge to assert one's individuality as a move away from those around one, and it may be, for it may be the rebellious substitution of a new set of rules for those of the social group, an act of rejection of social demands—and perhaps also of those making the demands. This is an isolating step. But the acceptance of personal responsibilities made possible by completed caring is not isolating at all; rather it signals acceptance of a uniqueness that has gradually been disclosed and apprehended, and the act of acceptance moves one closer to those who have nurtured the individuality and uniqueness. The act of acceptance is but a later stage in the growth of a person who has discovered his worth and gradually assumed the functions of the person who has that worth. It is his confident assertion that he knows what is important to him and thus what and whom he will support. It is in no sense a rejection of the "I must," but merely the shedding of the last vestiges of the "You must" in which it was first introduced. It becomes "I must because I want to."

Accepting a responsibility is a form of personal commitment. It follows from the decision to be the kind of person for whom this is morally required, or even "the natural thing to do." It may or may not be pleasant, or popular, or a source of gain, but it is an entailment of the self that is being actualized. Even if its necessity is regretted—because it gets in the way of other things, or involves actions that are not to one's liking, or carries a heavy cost—it is a part of becoming the person one chooses to be and exhibiting the qualities one insists upon having. The fact that it has been chosen as a part of the life that is fulfilling makes all the difference in the world in the spirit in which it is performed, the vigor with which it is pursued, and the effect it has on the moral development of the agent.

## 4.6   THE CHOSEN SELF

Although the self we first experience is conferred, the self which constitutes our own best self is chosen. It must be our choice if it is to express and deal with our cares and concerns. It must be our choice because only in this way can we make its moral necessities our responsibilities. But why accept cares and concerns? Why be responsible? Responsibilities are almost invariably onerous as well as gratifying, and so we must have a reason for choosing this particular self-in-process-of-becoming. Its qualities, skills, and arts must hold an attraction for us; its cares and troubles must be those we want to make ours, for we are insatiable in our urge to have as enjoyable a life as we can. To be the best person we can be, we must think that the life that person would lead is the most attractive one available to us. If this is not the case, we will not choose to be that person. No matter how "virtuous" we think that person would be or how "good" the works he might perform, we will not give up more attractive pursuits.

We seek what we consider most attractive, best for us, whether, being uncaring, we seek it in obtaining goods and services for ourselves, whatever the cost to others, or whether, being caring, we seek it in responsible living. In the former case, it will be less intense and more sporadic because such a person is at odds with himself. He is subject to the fissures Plato described: his pleasures conflict with his duties and his wants with those of others. In some important sense he cannot pull things together. We might say, in language that is figurative but revealing, that he has at least two selves. This comes close to describing the situation Plato described as universal. He presented it in the myth of the charioteer, who had the nearly impossible task of driving a span of horses, one of which wanted to go in the "right" direction and one of which wanted to go in any other. The former was noble and "spirited," the latter carnal and "unruly." Their incompatibility was never-ending, and the driver, whom Plato thought knew the rightful course to take, had a problem that would not go away. Plato's parable described what he took to be a constant feature of human nature. The driver was reason, and the horses were the emotions. Some emotions were supportive of virtuous, i.e., rational, living, and some were destructive of it. Reason could only prevail by beating the latter into submission, and that is what Plato recommended as a life of virtue.

We call this self-discipline, and we have doubts about its practicability. It is the central thesis of modern dynamic theories of personality that emotions, no matter how hurtful, are psychic forces we have shaped to meet needs of our own. Our feelings express what we "really" want or dislike. The Spanish philosopher José Ortega y Gasset, using poetic language to describe the way feelings operate, referred to the heart as "an acceptance and rejection machine," and he called it the foundation of our personality (Ortega 1959, 85). He was essentially correct, for our feelings structure our responses to everything we come upon. They cannot be ignored, for they provide our motive power. Nor can they simply be beaten down (repressed) or redirected by an act of will. They are always active. When they are destructive, therefore, they can only be redirected to a constructive role by being aligned with aims that are attractive.

This is possible because feelings are learned responses. The programming of the "horses" that move us is not biological and given, but psychological and conditioned. Feelings are not by nature good or bad; they become so in relation to the values that are brought to the fore in our development, which as we have seen, is emotional, social, and moral. They are not subject to command, but to cultivation. We respond from the beginning to accept or reject what is happening to us, but what we accept or reject is a reflection of the valuations we make.

We cannot, therefore, simply choose happiness. Our happiness is a concomitant of a larger choice, one which selects out those personal qualities and concerns that we think are important and worthwhile. What we are faced with, then, in deciding who we are becoming, and therefore what we must do, is making the choice that meets both our normative and our affective standards. The first judges our virtue, the second our happiness. When we find a way of life and course of action which meets both standards, we can expect a life in which what we find satisfying is worthwhile and what we find worthwhile is satisfying. It is that state of affairs which I said at the beginning I believe we all want and I believe we can all achieve.

When I made this claim, I was well aware that most people would think me outrageously optimistic, for this is just what Plato told us is impossible. But I also knew what companionate caring can do for those whose caring becomes habitual and characteristic. Then our concerns are caring: when we care for someone or about something, we find we must do something—and what we must do is what we want to do.

Companionate caring is the only attitude that performs this function. Caring, or its lack, is crucial in determining how our feelings will be related to the rest of our lives. If we are not caring, we remain at odds with ourselves. We accept duties and obligations but never internalize a justification for doing so. Doing what we "ought to" do does not engross us, for we are carrying out dictates originating elsewhere, conforming. We cannot "choose" who we will be; we retain the self conferred upon us by those who care for us but fail to nurture us. We are not engrossed in what we are doing, and we don't want to do it. Our desires and our aims are discordant. Our "horses" want to go in different directions, and our attempts to improve the quality of our lives feel like efforts to discipline ourselves. Our personalities are only partially and imperfectly integrated. We cannot bring things together in a concerted way: when we are doing what we like to do, we are not doing what we consider important; when we are doing what we think worthwhile, we are not enjoying ourselves. But this is not an existential state, only a failure of caring.

A chosen self, then, is a caring self. With a self we have chosen, we want the responsibilities entailed in the person we want to be. Our feelings and aims enter into a dynamic interplay in which each strengthens the other. Our feelings reinforce the resolve with which we pursue our aims; our aims are shaped by the reactions contained in our feelings. We enter into a feed-forward loop so that both the energies at our disposal and the concerns expressed in our aims are amplified. Our chosen self is a more energetic self, and it is directing its own course. Because the yes-no reactions of its feelings are clear and direct, we are able to correct our course as we go along so that life is more enjoyable. Because we are engaged in the engrossing activities of greatest concern to us, we are more sensitive and responsive to the possibilities of our lives and surroundings. We feel things more fully and deeply. In caring we adjust our lives so we can carry out our aims more successfully, fit them together better, discard those that are unrewarding, no longer fitting, or in conflict with more important ones, and modify them in light of changed concerns or circumstances.

To be caring is to live a life of amplified feelings. Our satisfaction reflects our positive assessment of its quality and success. In a continuous and searching appraisal, we judge how satisfying and practicable our aims are, how they promote or obstruct other purposes, and how they affect other people and our relationships with them. We proceed reflectively, using our best judgment. Our feelings are a key element in this continuing appraisal. As we go along, we test our aims against the satisfactions they make possible and the disappointments they bring us. Our passions and our insights play against each other. While we use our intelligence to devise our aims and find the means for reaching them, we rely upon our feelings to provide the motive power and local direction to our efforts. The psychiatrist Willard Gaylin states it well:

"feelings are the instruments of rationality, not—as some would have it—alternatives to it.... Feelings... are fine tunings directing the ways in which we will meet and manipulate our environment." (Gaylin 1988, 7) As we put our purposes into effect, our feelings register reactions to both their consequences, the life we lead, and to us, the agent in charge. They serve as indicators that we are or are not living in accordance with our own highest conception of what we can become. When we live in accord with our choice, we feel proud and competent and grateful; when we deviate from the course we have set for ourselves, we feel guilty, ashamed, irresponsible, incapable, insensitive. Both positive and negative signals help us stay the course; both success and failure affect a highly sensitized person.

It is clear that Plato was wrong. There is no natural and inevitable conflict between intelligence and feelings. He had a stunted view of both. Intelligence is the reasonable management of life, not simply recognizing the laws of logical implication; feelings are responses to life, not merely reflexes of fight or flight. There are many occasions—for example, when we are uncaring or self-seeking—when we do find our aims and feelings in conflict, but this is not inevitable, only regrettable. Ethical living does not require the suppression of natural feelings; moral aims and strong feelings can be mutually supportive. Feelings and intelligence begin their lives together, and they are both responding to the same world. When they both succeed in their functions, they reinforce each other.

The generative theory of personality has only slowly developed. John Dewey described personality in these terms. He pointed out that feelings themselves contain an interpretation of the experience to which they react, and he showed that this interpretation is in its very nature practical, the means by which we guide ourselves in a world which is constantly changing. Nel Noddings filled out that picture by describing a feeling which bonds people who are helping each other to develop in a self-chosen and unique pattern. Both Dewey and Noddings contribute to a worldview which is open and processual. Dewey substituted for the predetermined truths of "reason" the practical and value-laden creativity of "intelligence." Noddings substituted for the charity of those who know what is good for others the caring of those who nurture in others qualities which are chosen by the ones they cherish rather than by themselves.

There is no inherent and necessary conflict between feelings and intelligent ways of organizing our lives, nor is there an unresolvable conflict between what people find satisfying. Nevertheless, particular desires and satisfactions conflict, particular life patterns conflict, and particular desires conflict with particular aims. There is no grand pattern which fits all our aims and satisfactions together in a harmonious pattern which at the same time excludes frustrations, pain, and so forth. As we have seen, everything in nature is poised, off-balance, and jostling with other systems with conflicting needs which must also be recognized if not fully satisfied.

What we need to do, then, is to find out how an ethical way of life based in companionate caring influences both our conception of the kind of society which will be most supportive and the conception of character which contributes most effectively and fruitfully to community.

What we can expect of an ethics based in companionate caring influences both our conception of what a community is and what a person is, when both are viewed ethically. When we look, we find that each has been viewed from a new perspective in the modernizing western world.

# 5.
# Unique Personal Worth

November 7, 1998

We want to improve the quality of our lives, and it is now time to pause and consider what we can learn from these three apparently quite disparate sources that will help us in this effort. We can expect they will open up a radically different approach to life, since each of them breaks with western tradition in a matter central to it and, taken together, they challenge its entire perspective. They force scientists to reject the longstanding assumption that physical and biological forces are atomistic and mechanistic, psychologists to give up the notion that human nature is unchanging, and those concerned with the part feelings play in personal development and relationships to discard the idea that they are inherently disruptive. We are trying to develop a philosophy of life, and so we are concerned with the impact of these discoveries upon our understanding of the values which further the development of personality and the formation of character.

Philosophical discussions of such values have tended in the past to be utopian. They have tried to define moral perfection and to describe "the good society." These recent analyses of nature and personality, however, lead to the conclusion that in our world there is no such thing as perfection, perfect equilibrium, a perfect fit. Nothing is ever perfect and nothing ever gets perfect support from anything else. Everything is in a state of becoming because nothing is ever perfectly adjusted to anything else. Reality is an open-ended process in which the becoming of each is the endless interadjustments of all. Wherever we turn, whether to nature or the most intimate of personal relationships, we find a pulsating, networking reality, and the networking is effective because it coordinates energies contained in things and events which are forever slightly out of kilter with each other.

This being true of nature in general, it must also be true of us. We are natural beings: our energies are those that exist throughout nature, and they must, to be effective, have their impact in nature. Though, as we saw in the last chapter, they are organized in a way different from all other energies, they are not the less natural for that. The principle which applies throughout nature, we can expect, applies also to us: our relationships condition and limit our integration; our integration conditions and limits our relationships. Since, among our relationships, those with other persons are most formative and influential, we can conclude that to be more responsible, to contribute more or in more important ways to society, we must find satisfactions which are more worthwhile and worthwhile activities which are more satisfying, and to achieve a life of better quality, we must enter into more supportive relationships with others. Personal and social standards are not separate, but correlates of each other.

We are saying no more than that our effort to improve

things takes place in nature; it must make use of natural forces. We cannot be concerned abut the quality of our lives without realizing it is the quality of our lives we are trying to improve. Life is precarious, and so are our efforts to improve its quality. We live in a world in which hopes and aims are natural but vulnerable, in which improvements are always possible but never guaranteed, in which frustrations and failures are commonplace. We cannot even imagine a world in which everyone's needs are met, let alone one in which all their aims are accomplished. Our world is one in which trust and cooperation must be achieved by people who differ and disagree. What we can expect, therefore, is improvement, rather than perfection. And, since the improvements will be partial and what constitutes improvement will be redefined constantly, we cannot know what will be of greatest value in the future.

We do know, however, that we, human beings, will be the ones who experience and achieve those values. We will create the values and benefit from them. If worthwhile things are done, we will do them. If satisfactions are felt, we will feel them. What we are seeking is what will satisfy us and what we can find worthwhile. This is a profound change in perspective. We are not trying to fit ourselves into a perfect universe, but to find what is important to us. And this makes us important in a unique way. We have value on our own account. We have worth.

## 5.1   Value and Worth

Ethics has traditionally based its account of what a person should be and do in a theory of value. Plato made clear what this means in the Lysis, one of his early dialogues.

At the beginning of the dialogue, Plato pictured Socrates questioning the youth Lysis. Having ascertained that Lysis believed his parents loved him and wanted the best for him, Socrates asked him whether they permitted him his freedom—to ride his father's horses, prepare the family's meals, decide what he was to study with his tutors, and so on. Lysis admitted they did not, and the two of them finally decided it was not because his parents did not love him but because he didn't know how to do these things well. When he learned to manage such matters well, they concluded, his parents, and their friends also, would be only too glad to turn their affairs over to him. But then Socrates offered a sobering thought. When this happened, he suggested, they wouldn't be loving Lysis for his own sake, but for the skills he would provide—in other words, for the values he would contribute to their common life.

The conversation, with this conclusion, was a subtle attack by Plato upon Socrates' view that to be good is to be skilled, intelligent, wise in handling one's affairs. In criticizing such a position, Plato (for whom Socrates was speaking in this passage) seemed to be implying that loving someone means loving him for his own sake rather than for anything of value he may do, either for himself or for others. Yet Plato himself never provided a basis for thinking people should be valued for their own sake. In his social theory, as we have seen, he argued that a person is good to the extent he contributes to the common good, and in his personal ethics the soul which overcame bodily feelings, and thus made ethical living possible, was an alien power temporarily imprisoned in his body. A person might be important as the scene of conflict between good and bad, but he was scarcely someone to be "loved for his own sake." The good person was one who did well what contributed to the common good. The ultimate value was that common good.

But if we take seriously the caring feelings we have described as nurturing, we must conclude that there is something ultimately valuable in those we cherish. To use Plato's language, we love them for their own sake. What we offer them would not be nurturing if we did not love them for their own sake.

This feeling lies at the center of caring which is companionate, and it is a feeling which entails a judgment both about ourself and the other. The love we feel is deeply satisfying to us and at the same time a judgment that the cherished one is capable of making his life more satisfying and worthwhile and is open to the hurts and frustrations one comes upon in making the effort. Such a person, we can say, has worth.

We use the word "worth" frequently, perhaps most often interchangeably with "value," but here I wish to use both more precisely and as contrasting ethical terms. Anything is valuable which satisfies some need, want, or purpose. Water is a value when it irrigates fields or quenches thirst. In the first instance it achieves the purpose of the farm; in the second it satisfies the want or need of the thirsty person. But water is also of value—in theory or in retrospect—even if no one wants it, as was the case for millenia as it contributed to the chemical balances and cycles constituting Gaia, eventually our home. In its most general sense, value contributes something of importance to the situation in which it occurs. It is contributory; it is a value of, to, or for something other than itself.

Plato decided human beings were of value to the

extent they contributed to the common good. Lysis would be of value and therefore good if he contributed to the welfare of his family and city-state. Other ethicists have described the contribution in other terms and identified the contribution otherwise, but these differences are less important than the point of agreement, namely, that people are of value because they make a contribution of value to something of value. To ascribe worth to a person is to assert something entirely different. It is to assert that, in addition to any value they have, any contribution they may make, they also have value in themselves.

There has been a concept of worth in our tradition, but it came from religious sources which have never been melded completely with the classical ideas which dominated its ethics. Consequently, the tradition has been a complex amalgam of classical Greek and Judæo-Christian ideas containing inconsistencies in its value structure. Specifically, it was faced with the task of reconciling a secular theory which valued individuals according to their contribution to the common good with a religious tradition which saw them as equal in the eyes of God. According to the religious tradition, human beings, created "in the image of God," were of special concern to him regardless of whether they were good or bad, while our ethical theories claimed their value depended on their moral achievements.

In medieval times, salvation was "a gratuitous gift of God" given regardless of discernible merit (Aquinas 1947, I-II, Q109, A6, A2) Salvation was granted to some but not all human beings, and without apparent relationship to their virtue, thus blurring conceptions of merit and responsibility. It was not clear either what justified God's concern or that merit could be earned.

A change occurred in the Reformation, but not because the Reformers rejected the contradiction; in fact, they embraced it. But, even as they did so, they were led, largely by changes in society, to believe that God was subject to moral standards. This, while it did not resolve the contradition, recast the terms of the debate. Personal value was still balanced against the needs of the community, but now the community was the moral universe itself, a community in which individuals had worth which could not be taken from them. In this setting the contradictions became even more vivid and even more unacceptable. Furthermore, the standards of a rapidly modernizing world created ever more insistent demands for their resolution. Freedom, equality, and happiness were coming to be seen as reasonable expectations in a society in which progress was taken for granted. The value structure on which society rested had to be related in a positive way to personal merit.

What was needed was a philosophy of life—a theory of personality, of society, and of value—which would justify this. The philosophers of the Scottish Enlightenment attacked the problem in the eighteenth century, but they divided on the key issue. Adam Smith concluded that the pursuit of personal interests would enrich the community while David Hume decided that justice sometimes required that harm be done to the weak and virtuous. The latter contention so outraged the German pietist and philosopher Immanuel Kant, that, in his own words, it "roused him from his dogmatic slumbers." Kant took seriously both the religious and secular strands of the western tradition, and so was in a position to attack its inconsistenty. What he could not accept was the notion that we live in a universe in which virtue goes unrewarded. Accepting the Newtonian picture of the universe as rational and law-abiding, he argued that the laws which made it so also made it moral. Human beings, he asserted, are free, but their freedom lies in conforming to law, that is, a maxim which is universal and absolute. His formulation of that maxim was, Act so that your conduct can be universalized. Everyone would then be acting according to the same standard. This would be freedom for each and agreement among all. The needs of the community and of its members would be congruent.

Kant believed that his maxim, the categorical imperative, had several formulations, each of them deducible from the others. One of them was, "Never treat persons merely as means, but always also as ends." In saying that acting so your conduct can be universalized and treating others as ends are the same thing, Kant was attempting to merge the classical Greek and the Judæo-Christian traditions. He was taking a giant step forward in ethical theory by insisting that any adequate approaoch to life must provide a basis for respecting persons as persons, that is, must locate their worth.

However, he did not provide a satisfactory solution to the question, What is it about a person which constitutes this inalienable worth? He held that man is an "end in himself" and that "respect applies always to persons only," (Kant [1788] 1996, 109, 97) but he asserted that this respect is to be shown, not to the person, but "properly speaking, to the law that his example exhibits." (98) It is not the person, in other words, we are to respect, but the will he exerts in obeying this moral law, and ultimately it is the moral law itself which is to be respected. Personality inspires respect because it "sets before our eyes the sublimity of our nature (in its higher aspect)." (109) He differentiated this higher aspect from the lower, which he sometimes called animalistic. Despite his originality in other respects, Kant was still relying upon the theory of the divided self and, like Plato, calling for control of feelings opposed to complete rationality. Doing one's duty, he wrote, "produces by action (virtue) a consciousness of mastery over one's inclinations." The satisfaction which derives from ethical conduct is a "negative satisfaction." (109) This picture of subjective experience reflected Kant's allegiance to Newton's conception of nature as ruled by universal and absolute laws. Believing these laws justified moral aspirations, he had to conclude that human value derived from compliance with them. Despite his efforts, the ultimate value still lay outside human beings; they could not have "value in themselves."

Thus Kant, although he revolutionized ethical theory by claiming that all persons have worth, failed to identify in what it might consist. He tried to humanize a religious insight but ended stripping it of its content. Kant failed because he tried to identify the worth of persons in a static world, a world which had achieved the equilibrium made possible, indeed necessary, by absolute and universal laws. Kant's perfectionism required him to choose the timeless over the changing, and so he could not locate worth in human beings, the moral agents themselves. Newtonian physics with its implicit Platonic metaphysics blinded him. But we can take his dilemma as our clue to the solution of the problem: the universe is in process.

Human beings, as a part of nature and as having to fit into nature, are processual. If they are to be valued, it is for what they are doing, how they are doing it, and why they are doing it. But persons are what they are doing;

that is their being. They have worth in themselves. It is found in their effort to improve the quality of their lives, their effort to make their satisfactions more worthwhile and their worthwhile activities more satisfying.

They are enabled to do this by being nurtured; they make progress in doing it as they become nurturing. We described caring which is nurturing in chapter 2, but now we can consider it as an essential part of ethical life. Nurturing has a directive as well as an energizing function because a caring person ascribes worth to the persons he cherishes. This is apparent if we look at an experience in which caring of this nurturing kind is relatively uncomplicated by other matters. We love our own newborn child and think she has worth. What do we mean by this? We mean she is capable of deep satisfactions and vulnerable to hurt, capable of receiving and returning our love, and capable of having a satisfying and worthwhile life. We "know" all these things before she has provided us with any supporting evidence at all.

What we don't know is what is required of us in loving her and how she will express her love, what will prove satisfying for her, and how she will construct a worthwhile life. We don't know these things because they must develop out of her sensitivities and responses, and these will appear and be cultivated in our loving interactions with her. In them she will develop patterns of feeling, thought, and behavior which are uniquely hers. Knowing this, we approach her without reserve but cautiously. We are eager and expectant, but we don't know what to expect. We love her as she is, but we also love her as the person she will blossom into, a person we cannot even imagine in advance. Because she has weaknesses and shows promise, we support her in her efforts to have the life she finds satisfying and worthwhile and to be the person who can have that life. Because her satisfactions and worthwhile activities are unlike those of anyone else, she is morally unique and what nurtures her is different from what nurtures anyone else.

In caring for her companionately we do two things. We help her form her personality and develop her character. These have been treated as two different subjects in the past. Because our tradition has inherited the theory of the divided self, we have tended to treat personality as the locus of impulses and desires which may give us satisfactions but which need to be curbed by aims which are manifestations of character. But this cannot be true of a person who achieves an integrative-relational self. Those relationships which further integration and those integrations which further supportive relationships are to be fostered. This is what companionate caring does.

Let us, therefore, look again at companionate caring, this time stressing its ethical dimensions. Caring is a developmental process. In it both the worth we can achieve and the values we must create in order to achieve it become possible. Thus caring lies at the heart of ethics. It is the key to a philosophy of life which is both worthwhile and deeply satisfying. We can see this if we look more closely at the way in which caring relationships affect personality development and character formation.

## 5.2   The Conferred Self

Caring shapes personality because it begins before the self appears. Instinct plays a lesser role in human development than in the development of other animals and learning a greater role. This is because we human beings

are animals with a difference. All of our experience is
psychosocial: whereas other animals act and bond instinctively, we must learn who we are as we relate to each
other.

Our social milieu is especially formative because it
exists even "prenatally." Somewhere along the line of
species development, organic changes made possible a
different sort of creature. No one knows the sequencing
of these events, or their precise causes, but the general outline is clear enough. Arboreal primates came out
of trees to travel erect on open savannahs. For some
unknown reason the brain characteristic of the species
doubled in size, and this precipitated a crisis. The cra-
nium grew larger to contain the much enlarged brain,
while the pelvis remained unchanged in size and became
more restricted in child-bearing because of the new erect
stance. Birth had to occur at an earlier stage in the development of the fetus if the offspring was to survive.
The change was effected and the human infant has been
born "prematurely" ever since; if it went to term at a
developmental stage comparable to that of other mam-
mals, it would be born at about the age of two. But by
that time it is already well advanced along another path;
its emotional development has been influenced by its
socialization. Its physiological needs and its methods of
dealing with them have been incorporated in emotional,
intellective, and social patterns, what we call habits or,
when they are found generally in a culture, customs.

This late "prenatal" development is the source of "human nature"—with its more complex and less instinctual
feelings than those of other animals; its ties, of dependency, loyalty, and assertion, with others; its questioning,
investigative modes of response to surroundings; and its

sense of self—which differs so strikingly from the latencies of other animals. Its temperament, disposition, and personality are all created in its socialized integration. The infant seeks satisfaction by integrating its desires, but its desires themselves, some of which we call needs, and its ways of dealing with them are largely the products of its socializing activities. The integration and socialization of the emerging self are two aspects of one unity; like any natural event, the self is integrative-relational. Its personality is formed as it interadjusts with its social milieu; its relationships are shaped by its needs and desires. For human beings selfhood is a physio-psycho-social achievement.

What kind of personality and character we develop depends most importantly upon whether as infants we are cherished or merely tended. It was not until World War II, and then only because some orphans were housed in impersonal institutions of care, that it was discovered how important having affection and certain specific demonstrations of it are to the development of infants. Even when they received all the physical necessities, newborn infants wasted away and died within a matter of months if they were not cooed to, cuddled, fondled, and rocked. Because in other cultures and circumstances these forms of affection had been taken for granted, the "normal" development of infants was regarded as a working out of physical patterns that needed only the satisfaction of physical needs to place them in operation. Now we know how naive this view was. The development of feelings is essential to survival at this early stage, and they develop along with other aspects of personality in interpersonal interadjustments. What feelings are cultivated and how is of primary importance, and this depends in large measure upon what kind of caring infants receive.

If the caring is companionate, we perceive that things are done for us lovingly in response to our recognized needs. We are being cherished and being offered services. We are aware of both, and from the beginning we are as responsive to being cherished as we are to receiving services. Both are important, but how we think they are related is what affects us most. In companionate caring the cherishing and the servicing are bound together; neither can be separated from the other, and each is altered by being so bound. What binds them in this way is the judgment made by the one caring, the judgment that the object of his caring is a person who has worth. This means, as we have seen, that this as-yet-undeveloped being is sensitive and responsive, able to receive and return love, and capable always of achieving deeper and more durable satisfactions.

This is a strong imputation, and it cannot help but affect the way in which the simplest service is performed. Caring, to be companionate, must, from the beginning and, to the extent possible, always treat the object of caring as a person having worth. To say he is a person is to say he is an other, one with a life of his own; to say he has worth is to say that life can be both satisfying and worthwhile. To cherish a person in this way is to regard him as one whose satisfactions can become more worthwhile and his worthwhile activities become more satisfying. We are not, of course, describing any human relationship. We are describing an idealization of any human relationship. This is easiest to conceive as a relationship to a newborn baby, but any parent knows that his or her caring is less than perfect. Even loving parents are human beings. What is remarkable, however, is the power of the caring and the far-reaching effects of the ascription of worth at this very early stage in the development of personality.

By responding to us as persons as well as to our needs, caring others take the first step in creating a person. They bestow a persona upon us before we have a self of our own. The imagined self imputed to us is quite specific, and it evolves rapidly as those who confer it upon us modify their attitudes and actions to take into account our responses. We adjust to act the role we are given; it is that of a conferred self (Norton 1991, 161–2). We enter into an interadjustive relationship with our caring others, and our responses, as we begin to identify with our persona, both link us in bonds of affection and regard to those who cherish us and constitute steps in our own self-definition.

Our selves contain a self-evaluation from the beginning. We proudly accept the selves conferred upon us because they express the pride those who cherish us feel in us. The caring others communicate to us their sense of our worth. They cultivate our sensitivities by responding to them selectively and our responses by being sensitive to them, but they are not simply nondirective in this. They let us know by their sensitiveness and responses that we are worth satisfying and that our satisfactions are worth cultivating. Out of their awareness of our worth emerges our sense that we can have worthwhile satisfactions. It may seem curious that we are never entirely satisfied with who we are and are always trying to become something more, but now we can see why. In this most natural transfer, loving others wrap their dreams of a worthy person and a satisfying life in the self they confer upon us. From the outset the hope is as real as the actuality and a part of it; from the very beginning, we recognize that we are incomplete, and we have the urge to improve the quality of our life and our self.

This incompleteness of human beings, always combined with an almost ineradicable striving to become more competent and more worthwhile, has been noted by many, but no adequate explanation for it has been given. Our drive to improve ourselves and the quality of our lives is not organic, but personal, a product of caring. We develop our sense of self and our desire for fulfillment in response to the imputations of caring others.

Worth is not an abstract ideal, the same for all of us. It is unique for each of us, and emerges as we respond to those who cherish us. They give substance to the self they have conferred on us by assigning us a role. The role is very simple at first and much coaching is needed. The role is that of a happy person, and so we are pleasured in many ways. It is that of a much loved person, and so affection is lavished upon us. It is that of a competent person, and so we are given simple tasks we can perform well. It is that of a responsive person, and so our responses are elicited by cuddling and caressing us and tossing us in the air. It is that of an adventurous person, and so we are given tasks that call for the use of new skills. It is that of a responsible person, and so we are given simple duties. We grow into our roles and, treated always as persons who are comfortable in our role, we become the self for whom the role is natural. A self has been conferred upon us, and we have accepted it.

The self becomes more firmly ensconced and more clearly defined in further interactions that continue to build upon these early expectations and achievements, and, being adventurous and confident, we venture forth into the world. We become assertive. How do those who cherish us help us to choose a constructive path as we attempt to assert ourselves? They give us duties and some simple rules by means of which we can fulfill them.

The expectations of those who care are made clear in the assigned duties. The duties help to define the emerging self that is being conferred. They are our obligations because they are the natural functions of the person who has the worth imputed to us and who is playing the role assigned to us. They are given proudly by loving others who envision this worth as our promise, and we accept them with pride because we accept this loving assessment. The duties assigned are an expression of the caring; the caring others are defining obligations they are confident we will carry out, giving us assignments that will help us enter into their caring community. In chapter 2 we discovered that those who care feel an "I must" that contains both their feeling of responsibility for the one they cherish and their respect for him as an autonomous, responsible person. At this stage of our development they communicate their "I must" to us by assigning us duties ("You musts") they think are prerequisite to the development of our worth. Their "You must" becomes our "I ought to." We do what others think we should do. We obey rules.

At this stage rules have a constructive role to play. By obeying them we come gradually to visualize the person we can be and the worth we have. We cannot, in the beginning, understand the principles which justify the rules, and so we use the rules as a crutch while we gain insight. As long as our duties and the rules that enforce them are clearly related to the worth imputed to us, they serve as aids to our growing sense of self. We do what we "ought to" because we are the person who can be relied on to carry out these duties. We meet others' expectations because we accept them; by obeying the rules we satisfy both ourselves and the caring others.

But there is a natural tension here. The "I ought to" we accept as a part of our conferred self is double-edged. On the one hand, we are taught that we should seek satisfactions because we are worth satisfying and that we should become competent to make our own decisions about what life is worthwhile and how it can best be lived; on the other, we are taught that we should obey our elders and accept their judgment as to what our obligations are. Ultimately these two learnings clash with one another, in what may be the most dangerous conflict encountered in childhood. Unthinking conformity will interfere with the continued questioning and exploring required for self-discovery and the development of a sense of responsibility.

The tension can take either of two forms because there are two types of caring. We have been describing companionate caring and the effect of its ascription of worth upon the formation of personality. Traditional caring stands in contrast to companionate caring because those who care in the traditional fashion ascribe value instead of worth to the ones they care for. They see the one cared for as capable of experiencing satisfactions and vulnerable to hurt, capable of receiving and returning love, and able to make a contribution of value to others. It is this last ascription which differs from that made by one who offers companionate caring. It is an ascription of value rather than an ascription of worth, and it affects everything.

We recognize it immediately as an attitude consistent with the Platonic point of view. There is a common good in existence before the infant is born; the parents are the custodians of that common good, and their function is to instruct the child in what he must do to contribute to it. They confer a self upon him. It has value, and he is proud of it. It has a role, and he assumes it. It has satisfactions, and he takes pleasure in them. It has skills and he uses them. It has duties, and he performs them. A self has been conferred upon him, and he accepts it.

But there is a remarkable difference in this developmental process and in the self that has been conferred. The caring here is directive also, but in a different way. He has not been taught that his satisfactions can become more worthwhile and his worthwhile activities can become more satisfying. For him being satisfied is one thing and doing worthwhile things something else. He has two goals in life, and he must balance the two. He is urged to do worthwhile things, and he is told what is worthwhile. He may or may not find satisfaction in doing what he is taught is worthwhile. If he does not, he does what he is supposed to do but gets little pleasure out of it. If he does, it is the "negative satisfaction" Kant recommended, the pleasure one gets out of doing what he should do when he would rather be doing something else.

He still seeks satisfaction, but these are now divorced from what is "worthwhile." He seeks them because it is natural for us to do so. It is so natural that if what is pleasurable is different from what we think is good, we will probably seek gratification rather than responsible conduct. The only way to counter this tendency is to condition ourselves to find pleasure in doing good. Hence the puritan.

This kind of caring leads to the classical ideal of love which we know through Aristotle's theory of perfect friendship. Friends share in the good; they do what is good for each other. It leads also to the theory of the divided self, the notion that there are some feelings which are innately bad and which should be suppressed. And it leads to the notion that morality, in its most perfect form, involves merging the self into some greater or more perfect being or object.

If those in charge continue to assume our feeling-defining, response-formulating, decision-making functions, they intrude upon and weaken essential self-defining functions we must use to develop in a healthy fashion. They teach us that what they really expect is obedience, not development. Treated this way, our vision of the worth they have seen in us will become blurred and we will find it less compelling. They must remember that nurturing is not simply guidance.

The child learns the rules, accepts the obligations, defines himself as "good" to the extent he lives according to the rules, and discovers society to be a group of people who accept and live by a set of agreed-upon rules. He does what is expected of him (or rebels at doing it), plays a role, performs functions, carries out duties. But the role is assigned, the values are borrowed, and the duties are formal. He is acting out of a sense of obligation.

If this dutiful life becomes an end in itself, it can have tragic consequences, for then the imposed duties are generalized, stereotyped. This is always the case if those in charge are themselves guided only by rules and consider morality to be a life of duty, but it can also happen if caring others simply insist he live up to their expectations. In either case they are not sufficiently engrossed in his feelings to notice just what is troubling him or what gives him joy; they already have an idea what should be troubling or joyful, and they call upon him to live according to these idealized standards. They offer duties and obligations that have not been tailored specifically to him. They do not build on his particular competences, recognize his particular frailties and limitations, or use his budding aspirations. They assign duties and obligations that are not customized, and they fit poorly.

Anyone is sensitive enough to see when he is not the real object of attention and concern, and his responsiveness is stunted. What he sees in those around him is a blurred image of who he is and should be because they are projecting a stereotyped persona upon him and are not accepting him as he is. They cannot affirm his future self because it can only grow out of the present self they have not received and accepted. Since the vision they have for him is not tailored to his abilities and hopes, he can only see himself as a failure.

He can, however, recognize his duties. These take on greater importance in his relationships with others as the lack of their engrossment distances them from him, and he perceives the duties and rules he has been given as absolute and inflexible. They are not justified by his vision of who he wants to be, and so he must accept them literally. They have no special application to him.

He is confined to a world of rules, and there is nothing unique about him. He has entered into a framework of expectations in which he can carry out his obligations only by denying his own uniqueness. He can only feel good about himself and gain the approval of others if he follows rules he cannot justify. If, recognizing that he is somehow demeaning himself, he rebels, he gains the enmity or disapproval of others. If, currying favor, he does what he has been told, he becomes alienated from his own feelings. He is bound to be resentful, for he can see that neither what he receives from others nor what is expected of him has special application to him. His tragedy is personal: his relationships with others are deadened, and he is depersonalized.

This disconnection of rules from their justification in the necessities of growth is all too common. In fact, rules are generally used as short-cuts. They are posed as demands of "society" and placed upon the child by parents or their surrogates who serve only as messengers and enforcers. In such circumstances, the child subordinates himself to the demands of the group when he acts in accordance with the rules; when he violates the rules, he is asserting himself against the rigid controls of a constraining social group. It is easy to see here the origin of the traditional self-society split. The split is fatal, for any child sooner or later asserts himself against rules that he feels are foisted upon him. In a caring community, where rules are merely a way a child is helped to discover who he can be, this is a way in which he declares that the worth is his and he will be responsible for discovering and carrying out its necessities. But when the rules are ends in themselves, the rebel tries to assert himself by declaring his freedom from social controls as such. Both are seeking their individuality, but one does so within the community, the other outside his group.

The language here is important. For the rebel there is no community, only a group legislating for its members. It is not their caring he is responding to, but their power. This is social interaction, but it is power-driven. The relationships are not nurturing, but prudential. Changes are not developmental, but reactive, the self-seeking exchanges of isolates.

Rules are secondary, even in childhood, for the needs of children are developmental. To think of caring as the inculcation of rules or to express one's caring merely by imposing rules is to miss the best chance to instill a strong sense of personal worth. To the extent this is done, the good is defined as obedience to rules and virtue as pleasing others. Here, of course, we are back to the theory of the common good and the belief that every moral person must subordinate his own concerns to it. The dynamism of caring does not exist here; it has been smothered by rules. For many, moral conduct is nothing more than obeying the rules that define what is right, but rules, in the nature of the case, cannot constitute a satisfactory ethics. As we have seen, ethics consists of efforts to achieve personal worth. The moral necessities of such efforts are at least as great and as compelling as any rules can be, but they are of an entirely different order.

That process is cherishing, which in its most primal form—we shall later find it takes far more complex forms—has as its functional units the ones who care, the ones they cherish, and the community of caring and cherished persons. We need not look beyond the process for its source, purpose, or justification. These are all found in the satisfactions and fruitfulness of the process itself.

Our sensitivities open us to certain influences. An infant, for example, gets hungry, and, being unable to satisfy his hunger himself, is vulnerable. His sensitivity, combined with his simple sucking reflex, allows him to satisfy his need by nursing. The process is physical, affective, and, soon enough, intellective and social. With incredible swiftness the feeding, combined with other caring acts and psychosocial changes and reinforced by repetition, becomes an interpersonal event. Its meanings are social: both mother and infant are recognizing the other as a source of satisfaction. The mother from the start, and the infant soon enough, see both themselves and the other as needing and wanting satisfaction in the relationship and as capable of greater satisfaction than they already experience. Each modifies his conduct to make the interadjustment more satisfying. Some things work, some don't. The feedback is instantaneous and strong.

Each is a person to the other, and each sees the worth in the other. Each also finds value in the other, but even at this early stage it is possible to distinguish worth from value. The mother has value for the infant as a source of food supply, as a comforter, as a reliable support; she supplies much that is of value to the infant. What she supplies is not just physical necessities and comforts, but also emotional support, intellectual stimulation, and an other with whom the infant can interact. The values are multitudinous and variegated. Similarly, the infant, all unknowing, is providing values to the mother: a responsive but often challenging other whose needs and satisfactions are physical, emotional, intellective, and social. Its signals of gratification and frustration are patterned; the unity and design of the pattern is a clue to the presence of a person.

It is the detection of this person in the obvious gratifications and displeasures which is key to the discovery of worth. The worth is based in this capacity to gain satisfactions. In increasing and improving satisfactions, one defines oneself. A person as person is seeking to improve the quality of his life and can do so only by developing his sensitivities and responsiveness and making changes in his surroundings. He is dealing with the meanings he has given his experiences, attempting to meld them into a life which is more satisfying and worthwhile. Personal worth is the capacity to do this.

Values can be judged from many perspectives—that of the community, of some abstract principle such as justice, security, privacy, or profit, of any particular individual—but worth can only be judged in terms of the person in which it is found. The worth of two people cannot be judged on a common scale; each contains its own standard. Worth is incommensurable. This does not mean that every development which occurs in a person exhibits his worth; some blunt his sensitivities and responsiveness, and that is the test. There are commonalities in personality and experience, and this means there is an overlap between a person's worth and the values he creates and exhibits, but the two are not identical.

Thus we can go back to our tradition and its difficulty in explaining how a person can be an object of respect, even of love, quite apart from his morality. The answer is that each person has sensitivities and responsiveness which can be cultivated so that the quality of his life can always be improved, specifically, by becoming more satisfying and worthwhile for him. At the same time, this self-development occurs in a social context in which his conduct, beliefs, and attitudes must be judged by others as well as by himself. His value to others, to the community, even to himself, may differ from his worth.

Further, we can go back to the question we framed at

the beginning of this chapter, Why do we and why should we cherish someone? We cherish someone because we see his or her worth. That worth is accessible to us through our feelings: we discover it in his sensitivity and responsiveness, which we must receive from him. His "sacredness" lies in the fact that those sensitivities and that responsiveness can be nurtured and can nurture the same qualities in others. We cherish him because his sensitivities open him to our nurturing efforts and his responses, providing feedback to our overtures, provide us with satisfactions that are direct and can be intense. The interadjustments involved in caring are self-sustaining in an amazingly complex way.

The cherished one is being received and appreciated as a developing person, and the cherishing spurs him on in his development. Furthermore, the feelings and the actions that the cherished one stimulates are self-directing. The feelings communicated to the one cherished are those which allow him to perceive himself as worthwhile, deserving of appreciation, capable of doing things deserving of approval and support.

The process is integrative in at least three senses: the one caring is becoming more caring and a more caring person; the one cherished is unifying, relating, and integrating the feelings, hopes, and aims which make of him a responsible and autonomous person; and the interadjustments occurring between the two, described in some detail in general terms in chapter 2, create bonds between the two—and, where the caring is occurring in a group and involving several of its members, creating a community of concern.

Finally, the cherishing is self-generating. Its rewards are contained in it. The constant, strong, and mutual feedback gains force and becomes reinforcing. In many cases, the cumulative force is feed-forward. New energies are released in which all of those involved become more empowered.

Not all of the reactions are positive. Indeed, the most disruptive feelings are apt to occur in close relationships. A surprisingly high percentage of violent actions against persons are directed at those closest to the violent person—family members and those associated in projects regarded as important by the one who hurts the others. This testifies to the strength of the feelings involved in intimate relationships, even when these relationships are less than ideal. The relationships haven't ended; if they had, people would merely walk away from each other. In some sense the violent person cares, but he is hurt and doesn't know how to act constructively on his concern. This is a serious disruption of a caring relationship, however, and it calls to attention the fact that caring is self-corrective. The constant feedback provides clues as to what is supportive and what destructive, and, as long as we care, we can modify our behavior to make it more nurturing and more satisfying.

The generative quality is remarkable. First of all, the natural impulses which serve to initiate a caring relationship and respond to the first approaches are minimal. They are reflexes which are found in any normal newborn, but none of them is complex enough to provide positive feedback very long. Almost from the beginning, the ones that encourage the caring are made possible by developing feelings and muscles which provide no direction themselves. It is, indeed, the sensitivites which control, and these are elicited, given a direction, and shaped by the caring or cherished other. The neural development is so rapid that the responses of the parent have been regarded by many as maternal instincts. The truth is that human beings are "quicker reads" than we give them credit for being. We don't need instincts to respond caringly; we merely need to cultivate successful responses and make them habitual.

We can pinpoint the importance of caring by referring once again to an alternative explanation of what it is that gives guidance to our attempts to make our lives meaningful. Plato said that we have a soul which is rational—in fact, a fragment of a cosmic Reason which constitutes reality and makes it a cosmos, or ordered hierarchy. We can use our fragment of reason to control our feelings and order our own lives in an ordered human community. The soul, however, he thought, was only temporarily imprisoned in the body; it left the body at death. Nature and the body were not real—only that temporary resident, the soul, was. Any satisfaction to be gained by a person so described was purely intellectual, and it could appear only with the control and squelching of feelings. Enjoyment was not great, and it was not moral. Feedback from the feelings, where it existed, was negative.

This is not the way to ground moral conduct or to motivate people to be ethical. Puritanism is implicit in the approach.

Why should anyone be cherished? Why should a parent cherish his or her child? The question seems to be an especially "dumb" one in any of its variations. Why should a husband cherish his wife, or a wife her husband? Why, indeed, should one marry? Having described companionate caring, how do we justify it? Why should we be caring in our relationships?

We may ask ourselves the question in particular situations or with respect to specific people, but that is different. We may ask whether we should have children or whether we should marry. We may ask whether we want this person as a friend. Or, being married, we may ask whether we do in fact cherish our spouse. But in these cases we are asking whether another person does or would meet our standard for a friend, a marriage partner. The question I want to raise, though, is why anyone should be cherished, be an object of caring.

The question is not factual, but ethical—not why we do care, but why we should care. I mean to raise a question about us as human beings. Is there something about us as human beings which makes us worth cherishing? If there is, what is it? Or is there something about only some of us which makes us worth cherishing?

The answer to such questions lies right at the heart of ethics, and yet the questions are rarely discussed by professional ethicists. Even those who defend caring omit consideration of what it is about a person which justifies our caring about him or her. And those who do consider the matter do so in a fragmentary and superficial way. Perhaps they are frightened away, considering the topic a religious one rather than ethical. They may think it is enough to say there is something sacred about every human being or about every living thing. But this only points to something. What, if anything, is sacred about us? If we are sacred, how is this sacredness manifested?

The answer to this question cannot be simply in terms of the traditional theory of value, namely, that the moral excellence (or lack of it) of an individual is to be judged by his or her contribution to the common good. That view did not assign an inherent value to an individual:

it was the individual's contribution which had merit. On this theory some people were more valuable than others because their contribution was more valuable. Despite claims made by some forms of this theory, sacredness was not something which made everyone equal.

The pull of the religious vision was irresistible, however, and it finally became necessary to introduce into ethics a new concept. Let us call it personal worth. The concept, though not under this name, has a long history. Jesus' parable of the black sheep presents it in one form. The "black sheep," or sinful person, is worth the same concern as those who are blameless. One who has not demonstrated his value, in other words, warrants as much attention and concern as any other. Similarly, the parable of the grape gatherers. The one who comes late to the vineyard and works less than the others, deserves a full share when wages are distributed, for his need is as great. One person is, the message holds, as valuable as another, in spite of differences in their contributions to community life. This may be, as in these parables, a worth in the eyes of God, but Jesus offered it as a standard to be used in the community.

The theological and philosophical systems which have attempted to rationalize an assertion of worth to persons in addition to an evaluation of the value they have exhibited in their lives have been many. In Augustinian thought, those who were saved were distinguished from those who were not, and salvation came as a matter of grace from God. Protestantism altered this by stressing the notion of desert; people could, by their actions, become deserving of salvation, although the action was still, by most, conceived as an act of grace. Immanuel Kant, a pietist and rationalist, gave the greatest impetus to the introduction of the idea of personal worth into ethics when, in one version of the categorical imperative he believed contained the duty of all human beings, he declared that every person should be treated as an end, not merely as a means.

The pronouncement had the effect of complicating ethical theory. Since that time it has been necessary to find a basis for personal worth. Clearly, if people are in some sense moral equals, they cannot be judged only on the basis of what they have accomplished, whatever may be the standard of judgment of value.

Kant himself did not provide a satisfactory account of personal worth. It was not the person himself or herself who was, to his mind, the object of respect, but rather his or her obedience to the categorical imperative, that is to say, a rule of rational conduct he thought was written into the nature of the universe itself. This would not be enough. Worth, the dictionary tells us, is what is deserving of respect, and it is persons as persons, not persons as good or sacred, who deserve respect. That is the religious insight, and it is also the conception of human beings which was emerging as the western world modernized.

There is need for both a concept of value and a concept of worth in ethics, but their relationship could not be discerned and the latter gain meaning until a processual view of reality could be developed. In such a view personality is developmental. Both personality and character are conceived as unfolding. What they can become is as important as what they have become. Ethical conduct, without in any way becoming unhinged from its origins and past, is a way of shaping the future of both the agent and his surroundings.

Worth becomes the potentiality for creating value; value becomes that which a person of worth has achieved. The two are linked in a historical, personal quest.

It was a paradox of classical ethical theory that, though human beings made the choices and performed the acts which created moral values and although they gained whatever benefits accrued from those choices and acts, the value assigned human beings themselves was derivative. Their value lay in the contribution they made to the common good. The divided self, which we have found embedded in this classical theory, explained both how human beings could contribute to the common good and why it was so difficult for them to do so. The former capacity was found in their rationality, the latter limitation in their base feelings.

The Judæo-Christian tradition made a claim which contradicted this classical view. It asserted that human beings were themselves of value as the children of God. The claim varied in the several forms this tradition took, but all of the variants posed new problems for ethical theory: What is it that constitutes the merit ascribed to human beings? What are the personal resources by which it can be achieved?

In that form of the tradition which dominated western culture until modern times, the theory of the divided self was buttressed by the theological doctrine of original sin. Virtue required salvation, which was "a gratuitous gift of God" to human beings. Even before man's fall, wrote Aquinas, virtue was "infused" in him by God (Aquinas 1947, I-II, Q109, A6, A2) The denial of free will which this implied became increasingly objectionable in the modernizing world.

Immanuel Kant formulated an ethical theory designed

in part to overcome the objection, but it, too, failed in the end to locate value in human beings themselves. This was obscured because he held that one formulation of the rule that was universal and necessary for ethical conduct was that man, unlike the rest of creation, could not be used *"merely as means."* He justified this by saying that "respect applies always to persons only" and that man is an "end in himself." (Kant [1788] 1996, 97, 109) These assertions are often interpreted as meaning that Kant believed human personality has worth which is self-justifying and should never be violated. On this ground, he has been praised for making a turn in ethics toward a more modern and humanistic point of view.

On closer examination, however, the inference turns out to be faulty. Discussing respect, he wrote, this respect is to be shown, not to the person, but, "properly speaking, to the law that his example exhibits." (98) It is not the person, in other words, we are to respect, but the moral law which he accepts and obeys. Personality inspires respect because it "sets before our eyes the sublimity of our nature (in its higher aspect)." (109) This higher aspect is sharply divided from a lower aspect, which he sometimes calls animalistic. Kant was relying upon the traditional theory of a divided self introduced by Plato. Doing one's duty, he wrote, "produces by action (virtue) a consciousness of mastery over one's inclinations." (144) The satisfaction which derives from ethical conduct is a "negative satisfaction." (144) Virtue comes as one masters one's own inclination. "The person as belonging to the sensible world [of pleasures and causes] is subject to his own personality as belonging to the intelligible world.... Man, as belonging to both worlds, must regard his own nature in reference to its second and highest characteristic only with reverence, and its laws with the highest respect." (108) Again here, as in Plato's ethics, we have to choose between reason and feelings, duty and pleasure.

Yet, within this confining classical perspective, Kant introduced new elements consonant with the hopes emerging in the modernizing world. He was both an ancient and a modern. First of all, he admitted, though in a narrowly conceived way, that life must contain both satisfaction and worthwhileness. The first, he wrote, had to be the happiness "estimated as reason especially requires" and the second what is "good or evil in itself." Furthermore, the second must be uninfluenced by the first, distinguished from the first, and made "the supreme condition thereof." (80-81) Clearly, the satisfactions would be incidental, though important.

Second, he asserted what is implied in this attempt to judge ethical conduct by the experience of the person exhibiting it, namely, that everyone has personal worth which demands respect. His attempt to identify in what this worth consists and how it is exemplified followed from his continued acceptance of an outmoded theory of personality. That conception of personality has now been replaced by a dynamical theory of personality as integrative and generative. What is personal worth in people who are achieving a unity of intelligence and feelings?

## 5.3    Personal Worth

Personal worth is the capacity a person has to respond to nurturing by improving the quality of his life.

The worth a person has is to be distinguished sharply from his value. The latter is discovered by the contribution he makes to a common good.

Most ethical theories do not make such a distinction at all. They do not need a concept other than and different from value because the good is considered to be definable in the abstract and then be used as a standard of judgment in assessing the performance of any individual. Such concepts as the right and the good are fixed, conceived either as deductions from some account of reality or products of agreement among those who legislate for the community. Thus a person who does what is right or displays traits or performs acts which are good is ethical. The standard comes first, and the judgment follows.

But this is impossible in a world in process. There values emerge, most often as unpredictable novelties. We recognize this in our personal relationships and our own experience. Those closest to us, including ourselves, acquire characteristics, both good and bad, which we could never have expected from the time of birth. We may not notice this because we are constant attendants upon a course of events in which change is usually gradual, but we learn to live with this continually changing person. And always, we accept the fact that there may be further changes, and some surprises. We come to realize we can never take ourselves or anyone else for granted.

This is, of course, truer for those who are companionately caring. Their affirmation, as distinct from their acceptance, of those they cherish (including themselves) always includes an attitude of expectancy. The affirmation is of the possibilities that exist in the cherished one, possibilities he has for the further improvement in the quality of his life. We can now rephrase this expectancy as acknowledgement of his worth.

The worth exists whether recognized or not. Thus, even those who, having adopted an ethics of duty to fixed ideals or goods or principles, call upon others and themselves merely to conform to standards which they believe to be unchanging, themselves have worth. Worth is not created by a theory which recognizes its existence, although it is more easily and often realized in such a setting; it exists because persons are by nature constantly seeking to improve the quality of their experience and lives. Those whose philosophies of life do not acknowledge the possibility of improvement beyond scenarios already approved in current standards, may become anxious when they visualize a better life or fail to note the evidence that it is available or feel guilty if they snatch at it. The better life is more difficult to envision and more difficult to accept in those circumstances, but it is always there in some form as a possibility.

Personal worth is a normal feature of a developmental psychology. It is nothing more than the assertion that in a being who is never "completed" but always capable of further development, as we have already discovered human beings to be, the integration of feelings and aims can always be carried further.

This has been recognized in a number of recent theories, and growth, maturity, and health have been words adopted to describe this possibility. In many instances the words have carried a favorable connotation, even a moral connotation, but the basis for the connotation has not been clear. After all, growth can be in any of many directions and not all growth is healthy. As people mature, they often appropriate qualities and habits which are destructive, of others, themselves, or both.

This difficulty and ambiguity has not occurred, at least in so flagrant a fashion, in traditional ethical theories, because they have adopted a picture of the "good" person as one who is the outcome of proper moral education. But these theories are deficient in a more fundamtal fashion: they picture a closed universe and a fixed human nature. We now realize that pesons, like any dynamical natural system, are open-ended in their processes. The availability of choices increases the openness of experience for human beings. We have to ask how we should decide between those paths of development which are ethical and those which are not.

Here the analysis of companionate caring comes to our rescue. The nurturing which it entails has a direction contained in it. It furthers a process which is self-regulating and self-energizing. It supports choices— in both the ones caring and the ones cherished—which strengthen the bonds between them and strengthen the particular integration of aims, satisfactions, values, and energies which constitute the individuality of each of those bonding.

This particular combination of values is, furthermore, possible because it occurs in a process which does not require agreement or harmony. It creates a larger unity, but it is one of understanding—what we call a caring community.

## 5.4    PERSONAL UNIQUENESS

Recall again the beginning of Plato's dialogue on friendship, where Socrates is pictured penetrating traditional ethical theory to reveal one of its major weaknesses. Socrates and the young Lysis agree that once Lysis can manage his affairs wisely, his parents will be only too glad to turn their affairs over to him. But then, Socrates suggests to Lysis: They won't be loving you for your own sake but for the skills you provide.

Though in section 5.1 above, I framed this dialogue as a failed effort, this opening discussion is perfectly clear. It is only when Plato attempts to get around this conclusion that friendship is only a disguise for a mutual benefit arrangement that the argument fails. Plato's difficulty lay in the fact that he ascribed value to people but not worth. Their value lay in their contribution to the common good, and this was calculable. Small contribution, little value; large contribution, great value—and, no contribution, no value.

The religious teachings mentioned above fundamentally altered this view. They claimed there is something meritorious in everyone, regardless of one's actual moral achievements. This added value was a different order and could not be assessed in the same way. Kant called it infinite, meaning that it was beyond measure. Human beings possessed it from birth, and it neither increased nor decreased. In fact, it was not quantifiable, not of a nature which was subject to increase or decrease. Kant, in thus distinguishing worth from value, was confronting a problem which up to then had been intractable. The problem was one of respect. Why should we respect equally people whose contributions to our common life— however these were conceived—were vastly unequal? Why should we respect at all someone whose contribution was harmful rather than beneficial?

It was not enough to say that every person is sacred. That only focused the question: In what did such sacredness consist? What is its origin? How is it revealed?

Kant's answers to these questions, as we have seen, failed. In claiming that it consisted in obeying the moral law, Kant placed the worth in one's relationship to an ideal realm. It was not people who were sacred, but their obedience to a law which did not depend upon their obedience.

Kant's failure stemmed from his belief that ethics must involve rules which are universal and necessary. This was a view he inherited from classical ethics, and it was possible only because traditional ethical theories had to have a measuring stick by means of which value could be judged. In spite of the considerable originality Kant showed in developing his ethical theory, he failed to take one further step to make it consistent. He tried to force personal worth into a framework, and thus make it uniform. He wanted to make people morally equal in some sense, and therefore deserving of respect as persons regardless of the value they had demonstrated in their lives.

The intent was noble, but the effort to carry it out was premature. Western culture had not yet moved far enough so that the full implications of imputing worth as well as value to human beings was apparent. The full shift could not be made until it was recognized that worth cannot be judged by any standard outside the persons to whom it is imputed. That is what is meant by saying that persons have value in themselves. This value is worth, and it creates its own standard.

The historical origins of the idea of personal worth in religion are significant. The "sacredness" is a spiritual element in human experience, and this quality of person is essential to any ethics which makes character as well as conduct important. Because classical ethical theories had no place for this spiritual element in their account of the good life and because religion sought to ground it in a source beyond human experience, spirituality has been looked on with suspicion by secularists. This is entirely understandable: this spiritual element can only be incorporated effectively in our lives if it is described in natural and personal terms. Kant was correct in saying that God cannot be ethical because he cannot confront the obstacles that make ethical conduct a spiritual attainment. What makes it possible for us to be spiritual is our humanness.

This insight inverts the traditional ethical standard of judgment. Because value was a contribution to something external—the community—a standard could be devised for judging it. Every good person was like every other person in that he met this standard. Immoral people might differ because they could fail in different ways to meet the standard, but good people were standard issue.

This was increasingly problematic for modern sensitivities. It may have been regarded as spiritually satisfying in Plato's day to think of the soul as the seat of reason and to picture it as a fragment of unchanging and perfect reality transmigrating from body to body, but in our most intimate relationships we think of ourselves and others as different from everyone else. Those we cherish, we believe, are imperfect, needing us, and capable of responding to us as no one else would or could. We consider ourselves, also, as worthy of such caring and capable of such response.

Individuality is stressed in all other areas of life. Economics teaches us that worth is increased if our skills are differentiated; psychology reveals individual differences in physical features, traits, and skills; education elicits interests that differ among students. But it has been difficult to break the hold of traditional views in ethics: friendship is still viewed as Aristotle viewed it, as possible only among those who agree upon what is good—in theory if not in practice.

What is needed is a bold stroke: Each person is morally unique. The worth he has is unlike the worth of any other person. Further, this uniqueness is incommensurable. It cannot be put on a scale of values and be judged more or less worthy than the unique worth of any one else. This may be what Kant meant by saying that personal worth is infinite: Spinoza had used the word to describe God who, because he was infinite, could not be described or judged by finite creatures. But infinite means unbounded, and human beings are bounded. Worth is always a specific worth, even though not inferrable in advance from any set of facts.

It is better to conceive of human beings as developmental beings, responsive to nurturing, capable of moral growth. Every person has specific possibilities and specific limitations, but which are unique in the sense that they are incommensurable.


## 5.5　The Nurture of Unique Personal Worth

There is a direction in the spiraling of personal development.

The top-down inculcation of rules or passing on of procedures is the least part of caring.

Companionate caring is a dynamical process. It is an inherently bidirectional coupling.

Companionate caring cultivates unique worth.

Unique worth is achieved in caring.

# References

Note: Because their citation systems follow established conventions, works by Plato, which use Stephanus pagination, and Aristotle, which use Bekker numbering, are omitted here.

Ackley, S.C. 1948. "John Dewey's Conception of Shared Experience as Religious." Unpublished Ph.D. dissertation (Boston University)

Allport, G.W. 1939. "Dewey's Individual and Social Psychology." In *The Philosophy of John Dewey*, edited by P.A. Schilpp, 263–90. (Northwestern University)

Aquinas, T. 1947. *Summa Theologica: First Complete American Edition in Three Volumes*. Translated by Fathers of the English Dominican Province (Benziger)

Briggs, J., and F.D. Peat. 1989. *Turbulent Mirror* (Harper & Row)

Burnet, F.M. 1959. *The Clonal Selection Theory of Acquired Immunity* (Vanderbilt)

Childe, V.G. 1936. *Man Makes Himself* (Watts)

Cloud, P. 1978. *Cosmos, Earth, and Man* (Yale)

Davydov, A.S. 1985. *Solitons in Molecular Systems*. Translated by E.S. Kryachko (Reidel)

REFERENCES

Dewey, J. 1894. "The Theory of Emotion. (I.) Emotional Attitudes." *Psychological Review* 1: 553–569.

——.1895. "The Theory of Emotion. (II.) The Significance of Emotions." *Psychological Review* 2: 13–32.

——.1896. "The Reflex Arc Concept in Psychology." *Psychological Review* 3: 357–70.

——. 1916. *Democracy and Education: An Introduction to the Philosophy of Education* (Macmillan)

——. 1925. *Experience and Nature* (Open Court)

——. (1922) 1930. *Human Nature and Conduct* (Modern Library)

——. 1931. *Philosophy and Civilization* (Minton, Balch)

——. 1938. *Logic: The Theory of Inquiry* (Henry Holt)

——. 1939. "Experience, Knowledge and Value: A Rejoinder." In *The Philosophy of John Dewey*, edited by P.A. Schilpp, 517–608. (Northwestern University)

——. 1962. *Individualism, Old and New* (Capricorn)

Dewey, J. and J.H. Tufts. 1932. *Ethics* (Henry Holt)

Dewey, J. and A.F. Bentley. 1949. *Knowing and the Known* (Beacon Press)

Edelman, G.M.E. 1992. *Bright Air, Brilliant Fire* (Basic Books)

Gaylin, W. 1988. *Feelings: Our Vital Signs* (Perennial Library)

Hempel, C. 1964. *Aspects of Scientific Explanation* (Free Press)

Hertz, H. 1899. *The Principles of Mechanics*. Translated by D.E. Jones and J.T. Walley (Macmillan)

Hochachka, P., and G.N. Somero. 1984. *Biochemical Adaptation* (Princeton)

Hodgson, M.G.S. (1958) 1974. *The Venture of Islam*. 3 vols. (Chicago)

James, W. 1890. *Principles of Psychology*. 2 vols. (Henry Holt)

Kant, I. (1788) 1996. *Critique of Practical Reason*. Translated by T.K. Abbott (Prometheus Books)

Lamprecht, I. and A.I. Zotin. 1978. *Thermodynamics of Biological Processes* (de Gruyter)

Locke, J. (1690) 1960. *John Locke: Two Treatises of Government*. Edited with an introduction and notes by Peter Laslett (Cambridge)

MacIntyre, A. 1988. *Whose Justice? Which Rationality?* (Notre Dame)

Mill, J.S. 1864. *Utilitarianism* (Longman, Green, Longman, Roberts, and Green)

Nicolas, G., and I. Prigogine. 1977. *Self-Organization in Nonequilibrium Systems* (Wiley & Sons)

Noddings, N. 1984. *Caring: A Feminine Approach to Ethics and Moral Education* (California)

Norton, D.L. 1991. *Democracy and Moral Development* (California)

Ortega y Gasset, J. 1959. *On Love: Aspects of a Single Theme* (Victor Gollancz)

Reiner, J. 1968. *The Organism as an Adaptive Control System* (Prentice-Hall)

Rogers, C. 1961. *On Becoming a Person: A Therapist's View of Psychotherapy* (Houghton Mifflin)

Rosen, R. 1987. "Some Epistemological Issues in Physics and Biology." In *Quantum Implications: Essays in Honour of David Bohm*, edited by B.J. Hiley and F.D. Peat (Routledge)

Ryle, G. 1949. *The Concept of Mind* (Hutchinson)

Smith, A. (1776) 1998. *An Inquiry into the Nature and Causes of the Wealth of Nations*. Edited with an introduction and notes by Kathryn Sutherland (Oxford)

Suppe, F., ed. 1977. *The Structure of Scientific Theories* (Illinois)

Tauber, A.I., ed. 1991. *Organism and the Origins of Self* (Springer Netherlands)

Varela, F. 1979. *Principles of Biological Autonomy* (Elsevier North Holland)

Varela, F., E. Thompson, and E. Rosch. 1991. *The Embodied Mind* (MIT)

Westfall, R. 1977. *Force in Newton's Physics: The Science of Dynamics in the Seventeenth Century* (American Elsevier)

Zotin, A.I. 1978. "The Second Law, Negentropy, Thermodynamics of Linear Irreversible Processes." In *Thermodynamics of Biological Processes*, edited by I. Lamprecht and A.I. Zotin, 19–30 (de Gruyter)

Zotrin, A.I., and V.A. Kanoplev. 1978. "Direction of the Evolutionary Progress of Organisms." In *Thermodynamics of Biological Processes*, edited by I. Lamprecht and A.I. Zotin, 341–348 (de Gruyter)

# Index